William Shakespeare

THE TEMPEST

Edited by Martin Butler

PENGUIN BOOKS

PENGUIN BOOKS

Published by the Penguin Group
Penguin Books Ltd, 80 Strand, London WC2R ORL, England
Penguin Group (USA) Inc., 375 Hudson Street, New York, New York 10014, USA
Penguin Group (Canada), 90 Eglinton Avenue East, Suite 700, Toronto, Ontario, Canada M4P 2Y3
(a division of Pearson Penguin Canada Inc.)
Penguin Ireland, 25 St Stephen's Green, Dublin 2, Ireland (a division of Penguin Books Ltd)
Penguin Group (Australia), 250 Camberwell Road, Camberwell, Victoria 3124, Australia
(a division of Pearson Australia Group Pty Ltd)
Penguin Books India Pvt Ltd, 11 Community Centre, Panchsheel Park, New Delhi – 110 017, India
Penguin Group (NZ), 67 Apollo Drive, Mairangi Bay, Auckland 1310, New Zealand
(a division of Pearson New Zealand Ltd)
Penguin Books (South Africa) (Pty) Ltd, 24 Sturdee Avenue, Rosebank 2196, South Africa

Penguin Books Ltd, Registered Offices: 80 Strand, London WC2R ORL, England

www.penguin.com

First published in the Penguin Shakespeare series 2007

Introduction, Further Reading, Account of the Text and Commentary copyright © Martin Butler, 2007
General Introduction and Chronology copyright © Stanley Wells, 2005

Set in 11.5/12.5 PostScript Monotype Fournier
Typeset by Palimpsest Book Production Limited, Grangemouth, Stirlingshire
Printed in England by Clays Ltd, St Ives plc

ISBN: 978-0-141-01664-1

Contents

General Introduction

Every play by Shakespeare is unique. This is part of his greatness. A restless and indefatigable experimenter, he moved with a rare amalgamation of artistic integrity and dedicated professionalism from one kind of drama to another. Never shackled by convention, he offered his actors the alternation between serious and comic modes from play to play, and often also within the plays themselves, that the repertory system within which he worked demanded, and which provided an invaluable stimulus to his imagination. Introductions to individual works in this series attempt to define their individuality. But there are common factors that underpin Shakespeare's career.

Nothing in his heredity offers clues to the origins of his genius. His upbringing in Stratford-upon-Avon, where he was born in 1564, was unexceptional. His mother, born Mary Arden, came from a prosperous farming family. Her father chose her as his executor over her eight sisters and his four stepchildren when she was only in her late teens, which suggests that she was of more than average practical ability. Her husband John, a glover, apparently unable to write, was nevertheless a capable businessman and loyal townsfellow, who seems to have fallen on relatively hard times in later life. He would have been brought up as a Catholic, and may have retained

Catholic sympathies, but his son subscribed publicly to Anglicanism throughout his life.

The most important formative influence on Shakespeare was his school. As the son of an alderman who became bailiff (or mayor) in 1568, he had the right to attend the town's grammar school. Here he would have received an education grounded in classical rhetoric and oratory, studying authors such as Ovid, Cicero and Quintilian, and would have been required to read, speak, write and even think in Latin from his early years. This classical education permeates Shakespeare's work from the beginning to the end of his career. It is apparent in the self-conscious classicism of plays of the early 1590s such as the tragedy of *Titus Andronicus*, *The Comedy of Errors*, and the narrative poems *Venus and Adonis* (1592–3) and *The Rape of Lucrece* (1593–4), and is still evident in his latest plays, informing the dream visions of *Pericles* and *Cymbeline* and the masque in *The Tempest*, written between 1607 and 1611. It inflects his literary style throughout his career. In his earliest writings the verse, based on the ten-syllabled, five-beat iambic pentameter, is highly patterned. Rhetorical devices deriving from classical literature, such as alliteration and antithesis, extended similes and elaborate wordplay, abound. Often, as in *Love's Labour's Lost* and *A Midsummer Night's Dream*, he uses rhyming patterns associated with lyric poetry, each line self-contained in sense, the prose as well as the verse employing elaborate figures of speech. Writing at a time of linguistic ferment, Shakespeare frequently imports Latinisms into English, coining words such as abstemious, addiction, incarnadine and adjunct. He was also heavily influenced by the eloquent translations of the Bible in both the Bishops' and the Geneva versions. As his experience grows, his verse and prose become more supple, the patterning less apparent, more ready to accommodate the rhythms of ordinary speech, more colloquial in diction, as in the speeches of the Nurse in *Romeo and Juliet*, the characterful prose of Falstaff and Hamlet's soliloquies. The effect is of increasing psychological realism, reaching its greatest heights in *Hamlet*, *Othello*, *King Lear*, *Macbeth* and *Antony and Cleopatra*. Gradually he discovered ways of adapting the regular beat of the pentameter to make it an infinitely flexible instrument for matching thought with feeling. Towards the end of his career, in plays such as *The Winter's Tale*, *Cymbeline* and *The Tempest*, he adopts a more highly mannered style, in keeping with the more overtly symbolical and emblematical mode in which he is writing.

So far as we know, Shakespeare lived in Stratford till after his marriage to Anne Hathaway, eight years his senior, in 1582. They had three children: a daughter, Susanna, born in 1583 within six months of their marriage, and twins, Hamnet and Judith, born in 1585. The next seven years of Shakespeare's life are virtually a blank. Theories that he may have been, for instance, a schoolmaster, or a lawyer, or a soldier, or a sailor, lack evidence to support them. The first reference to him in print, in Robert Greene's pamphlet *Greene's Groatsworth of Wit* of 1592, parodies a line from *Henry VI, Part III*, implying that Shakespeare was already an established playwright. It seems likely that at some unknown point after the birth of his twins he joined a theatre company and gained experience as both actor and writer in the provinces and London. The London theatres closed because of plague in 1593 and 1594; and during these years, perhaps recognizing the need for an alternative career, he wrote and published the narrative poems *Venus and Adonis* and *The Rape of Lucrece*. These are the only works we can be

certain that Shakespeare himself was responsible for
putting into print. Each bears the author's dedication to
Henry Wriothesley, Earl of Southampton (1573–1624),
the second in warmer terms than the first. Southampton,
younger than Shakespeare by ten years, is the only person
to whom he personally dedicated works. The Earl may
have been a close friend, perhaps even the beautiful and
adored young man whom Shakespeare celebrates in his
Sonnets.

The resumption of playing after the plague years saw
the founding of the Lord Chamberlain's Men, a company
to which Shakespeare was to belong for the rest of his
career, as actor, shareholder and playwright. No other
dramatist of the period had so stable a relationship with a
single company. Shakespeare knew the actors for whom
he was writing and the conditions in which they performed.
The permanent company was made up of around twelve
to fourteen players, but one actor often played more than
one role in a play and additional actors were hired as
needed. Led by the tragedian Richard Burbage (1568–1619)
and, initially, the comic actor Will Kemp (d. 1603), they
rapidly achieved a high reputation, and when King James
I succeeded Queen Elizabeth I in 1603 they were renamed
as the King's Men. All the women's parts were played by
boys; there is no evidence that any female role was ever
played by a male actor over the age of about eighteen.
Shakespeare had enough confidence in his boys to write
for them long and demanding roles such as Rosalind (who,
like other heroines of the romantic comedies, is disguised
as a boy for much of the action) in *As You Like It*, Lady
Macbeth and Cleopatra. But there are far more fathers
than mothers, sons than daughters, in his plays, few if any
of which require more than the company's normal comple-
ment of three or four boys.

The company played primarily in London's public playhouses – there were almost none that we know of in the rest of the country – initially in the Theatre, built in Shoreditch in 1576, and from 1599 in the Globe, on Bankside. These were wooden, more or less circular structures, open to the air, with a thrust stage surmounted by a canopy and jutting into the area where spectators who paid one penny stood, and surrounded by galleries where it was possible to be seated on payment of an additional penny. Though properties such as cauldrons, stocks, artificial trees or beds could indicate locality, there was no representational scenery. Sound effects such as flourishes of trumpets, music both martial and amorous, and accompaniments to songs were provided by the company's musicians. Actors entered through doors in the back wall of the stage. Above it was a balconied area that could represent the walls of a town (as in *King John*), or a castle (as in *Richard II*), and indeed a balcony (as in *Romeo and Juliet*). In 1609 the company also acquired the use of the Blackfriars, a smaller, indoor theatre to which admission was more expensive, and which permitted the use of more spectacular stage effects such as the descent of Jupiter on an eagle in *Cymbeline* and of goddesses in *The Tempest*. And they would frequently perform before the court in royal residences and, on their regular tours into the provinces, in non-theatrical spaces such as inns, guildhalls and the great halls of country houses.

Early in his career Shakespeare may have worked in collaboration, perhaps with Thomas Nashe (1567–*c*. 1601) in *Henry VI, Part I* and with George Peele (1556–96) in *Titus Andronicus*. And towards the end he collaborated with George Wilkins (*fl*. 1604–8) in *Pericles*, and with his younger colleagues Thomas Middleton (1580–1627), in *Timon of Athens*, and John Fletcher (1579–1625), in *Henry*

VIII, *The Two Noble Kinsmen* and the lost play *Cardenio*. Shakespeare's output dwindled in his last years, and he died in 1616 in Stratford, where he owned a fine house, New Place, and much land. His only son had died at the age of eleven, in 1596, and his last descendant died in 1670. New Place was destroyed in the eighteenth century but the other Stratford houses associated with his life are maintained and displayed to the public by the Shakespeare Birthplace Trust.

One of the most remarkable features of Shakespeare's plays is their intellectual and emotional scope. They span a great range from the lightest of comedies, such as *The Two Gentlemen of Verona* and *The Comedy of Errors*, to the profoundest of tragedies, such as *King Lear* and *Macbeth*. He maintained an output of around two plays a year, ringing the changes between comic and serious. All his comedies have serious elements: Shylock, in *The Merchant of Venice*, almost reaches tragic dimensions, and *Measure for Measure* is profoundly serious in its examination of moral problems. Equally, none of his tragedies is without humour: Hamlet is as witty as any of his comic heroes, *Macbeth* has its Porter, and *King Lear* its Fool. His greatest comic character, Falstaff, inhabits the history plays and *Henry V* ends with a marriage, while *Henry VI, Part III*, *Richard II* and *Richard III* culminate in the tragic deaths of their protagonists.

Although in performance Shakespeare's characters can give the impression of a superabundant reality, he is not a naturalistic dramatist. None of his plays is explicitly set in his own time. The action of few of them (except for the English histories) is set even partly in England (exceptions are *The Merry Wives of Windsor* and the Induction to *The Taming of the Shrew*). Italy is his favoured location. Most of his principal story-lines derive from printed writings; but the structuring and translation of these narratives into dramatic terms is Shakespeare's own, and he invents much additional material. Most of the plays contain elements of myth and legend, and many derive from ancient or more recent history or from romantic tales of ancient times and faraway places. All reflect his reading, often in close detail. Holinshed's *Chronicles* (1577, revised 1587), a great compendium of English, Scottish and Irish history, provided material for his English history plays. The *Lives of the Noble Grecians and Romans* by the Greek writer Plutarch, finely translated into English from the French by Sir Thomas North in 1579, provided much of the narrative material, and also a mass of verbal detail, for his plays about Roman history. Some plays are closely based on shorter individual works: *As You Like It*, for instance, on the novel *Rosalynde* (1590) by his near-contemporary Thomas Lodge (1558–1625), *The Winter's Tale* on *Pandosto* (1588) by his old rival Robert Greene (1558–92) and *Othello* on a story by the Italian Giraldi Cinthio (1504–73). And the language of his plays is permeated by the Bible, the Book of Common Prayer and the proverbial sayings of his day.

Shakespeare was popular with his contemporaries, but his commitment to the theatre and to the plays in performance is demonstrated by the fact that only about half of his plays appeared in print in his lifetime, in slim paperback volumes known as quartos, so called because they were made from printers' sheets folded twice to form four leaves (eight pages). None of them shows any sign that he was involved in their publication. For him, performance was the primary means of publication. The most frequently reprinted of his works were the non-dramatic poems – the erotic *Venus and Adonis* and the more moralistic *The Rape of Lucrece*. The *Sonnets*, which appeared in 1609, under his name but possibly without his consent, were less successful, perhaps because the vogue for sonnet sequences, which peaked in the 1590s, had passed by then. They were not reprinted until 1640, and then only in garbled form along with poems by other writers. Happily, in 1623, seven years after he died, his colleagues John Heminges (1556–1630) and Henry Condell (d. 1627) published his collected plays, including eighteen that had not previously appeared in print, in the first Folio, whose name derives from the fact that the printers' sheets were folded only once to produce two leaves (four pages). Some of the quarto editions are badly printed, and the fact that some plays exist in two, or even three, early versions creates problems for editors. These are discussed in the Account of the Text in each volume of this series.

Shakespeare's plays continued in the repertoire until the Puritans closed the theatres in 1642. When performances resumed after the Restoration of the monarchy in 1660 many of the plays were not to the taste of the times, especially because their mingling of genres and failure to meet the requirements of poetic justice offended against the dictates of neoclassicism. Some, such as *The Tempest* (changed by John Dryden and William Davenant in 1667 to suit contemporary taste), *King Lear* (to which Nahum Tate gave a happy ending in 1681) and *Richard III* (heavily adapted by Colley Cibber in 1700 as a vehicle for his own talents), were extensively rewritten; others fell into neglect. Slowly they regained their place in the repertoire, and they continued to be reprinted, but it was not until the great actor David Garrick (1717–79) organized a spectacular jubilee in Stratford in 1769 that Shakespeare began to be regarded as a transcendental genius. Garrick's idolatry prefigured the enthusiasm of critics such as Samuel Taylor Coleridge (1772–1834) and William Hazlitt (1778–1830). Gradually Shakespeare's reputation spread abroad, to Germany, America, France and to other European countries.

During the nineteenth century, though the plays were generally still performed in heavily adapted or abbreviated versions, a large body of scholarship and criticism began to amass. Partly as a result of a general swing in education away from the teaching of Greek and Roman texts and towards literature written in English, Shakespeare became the object of intensive study in schools and universities. In the theatre, important turning points were the work in England of two theatre directors, William Poel (1852–1934) and his disciple Harley Granville-Barker (1877–1946), who showed that the application of knowledge, some of it newly acquired, of early staging conditions to performance of the plays could render the original texts viable in terms of the modern theatre. During the twentieth century appreciation of Shakespeare's work, encouraged by the availability of audio, film and video versions of the plays, spread around the world to such an extent that he can now be claimed as a global author.

The influence of Shakespeare's works permeates the English language. Phrases from his plays and poems – 'a tower of strength', 'green-eyed jealousy', 'a foregone conclusion' – are on the lips of people who may never have read him. They have inspired composers of songs, orchestral music and operas; painters and sculptors; poets, novelists and film-makers. Allusions to him appear in pop songs, in advertisements and in television shows. Some of his characters – Romeo and Juliet, Falstaff, Shylock and Hamlet – have acquired mythic status. He is valued for his humanity, his psychological insight, his wit and humour, his lyricism, his mastery of language, his ability to excite, surprise, move and, in the widest sense of the word, entertain audiences. He is the greatest of poets, but he is essentially a dramatic poet. Though his plays have much to offer to readers, they exist fully only in performance. In these volumes we offer individual introductions, notes on language and on specific points of the text, suggestions for further reading and information about how each work has been edited. In addition we include accounts of the ways in which successive generations of interpreters and audiences have responded to challenges and rewards offered by the plays. The Penguin Shakespeare series aspires to remove obstacles to understanding and to make pleasurable the reading of the work of the man who has done more than most to make us understand what it is to be human.

Stanley Wells

The Chronology of
Shakespeare's Works

A few of Shakespeare's writings can be fairly precisely dated. An allusion to the Earl of Essex in the chorus to Act V of *Henry V*, for instance, could only have been written in 1599. But for many of the plays we have only vague information, such as the date of publication, which may have occurred long after composition, the date of a performance, which may not have been the first, or a list in Francis Meres's book *Palladis Tamia*, published in 1598, which tells us only that the plays listed there must have been written by that year. The chronology of the early plays is particularly difficult to establish. Not everyone would agree that the first part of *Henry VI* was written after the third, for instance, or *Romeo and Juliet* before *A Midsummer Night's Dream*. The following table is based on the 'Canon and Chronology' section in *William Shakespeare: A Textual Companion*, by Stanley Wells and Gary Taylor, with John Jowett and William Montgomery (1987), where more detailed information and discussion may be found.

The Two Gentlemen of Verona	1590–91
The Taming of the Shrew	1590–91
Henry VI, Part II	1591
Henry VI, Part III	1591

Introduction

MIRANDA	O wonder!

How many goodly creatures are there here!
How beauteous mankind is! O brave new world,
That has such people in't!

| PROSPERO | 'Tis new to thee. (V.1.181–4) |

This famous exchange encapsulates the ambivalence that runs all the way through *The Tempest*. Miranda's amazement at seeing her first group of European men is the moment at which the play's interest in marvels and strange sights reaches its culmination. Awe-struck by people from a western world that she encounters literally for the first time, Miranda finds visions opening up beyond anything she has previously known. All her preconceptions are challenged, and she is momentarily overwhelmed by excitement at the possibilities rising before her. A similar astonishment at the island has already been voiced by the European visitors, albeit for different reasons. For them, too, estrangement from their normal lives forces a reassessment that makes them see the everyday world as if through new eyes. In such circumstances, even the most commonplace object suddenly appears miraculous. 'How lush and lusty the grass looks!' exclaims Gonzalo (II.1.55), as if he had never walked on a lawn before.

Yet Miranda's outburst of wonder is countered by Prospero, who knows how this meeting has come about and cannot greet it with the same delight. There are many ways that his four monosyllables can be handled in the theatre. Sometimes they pass almost unnoticed, a moment of inscape that hints at private weariness distancing him from the public joy. At other times, his disagreement sounds more decisive, making Miranda appear naively innocent, her optimism a cruel illusion. After all, it is not a new world which she is discovering but the same old Europe. Or sometimes the voices of father and daughter are more equally weighted, as diverging responses to the same event. Neither character has the whole story, and together they gesture at uncertainties that reverberate beyond the end of the play. What is essential in every production is the dialogue between illusion and dis-illusion, which is so distinctive to the play's effect. The imaginative power of *The Tempest*'s enchantments – its marvels and miracles and picture of life as we would like it to be – is always in tension with the equally powerful disenchantment paradoxically emanating from the man responsible for all the magic.

In *The Tempest* Shakespeare engages with that taste for wonder, marvels and the exotic which was so frequent a strain in the drama of his time. Dozens of Elizabethan and Jacobean plays send their characters on journeys to faraway places, or engage them in actions that present possibilities unimaginable at home. Typical are plays like Thomas Heywood's *The Four Prentices of London* (*c.* 1600), whose heroes' adventures take them from city shops to the Middle East, or John Fletcher's *The Island Princess* (1621), a tale of love, heroism and betrayal set amongst European traders in the East Indies. Other plays bring into familiar environments characters who challenge the audience's sense of what is normal, like Marlowe's Tamburlaine or Shakespeare's Othello, putting the homely and the 'monstrous' into immediate contact. Such stories register the expanding geographical horizons of the day and their consequences for the mental horizons of the London theatregoer, the way that the age's burgeoning trade and discovery caused an answering transformation in people's ideas and self-image.

The Tempest captures this sense of infinite opportunity meeting infinite uncertainty. Set on an island somewhere between Italy and North Africa, it is located on one of the Mediterranean's busiest trade routes, and also at Europe's southern boundary, the place where the western world loses its dominance and shades into cultures that seem challenging and alien. Voyaging out of Italy to marry Alonso's daughter, Claribel, to the King of Tunis, the representatives of old Europe find themselves unexpectedly at the edge of the familiar. They lose their power of self-determination but acquire a perspective on their former lives that they could not have achieved at home. Their journey to the margins puts a question mark over the society from which they come, and causes a radical reassessment of the values by which they live and the kind of life to which they will return. What they take for 'normal' no longer seems so obvious or secure.

Of the many strange worlds in Renaissance drama, *The Tempest* has much the strangest. No other play creates a space which runs so entirely according to its own laws. The island setting – with its sharp boundaries, and magic that works here but nowhere else – makes its world seem isolated and self-sufficient, an autonomous theatrical laboratory with its own internal logic. It is populated by unique creatures who are difficult to account for within the usual rules of biology. No other play so profoundly unsettles the border between the human and non-human, which most fictions take for granted. Many plays have enchanters and spirits, but no spirit has such a complex personality as Ariel, while Caliban is a creature made completely from Shakespeare's imagination, compounded of many different species and fitting into no single category of animal or mankind. These figures call into question the lines by which human identity is normally marked out, and when they arouse pity, sympathy or fear, they force us to reconsider what we suppose are the limits of the human. Little wonder that in modern times the story has been transferred to a distant galaxy peopled by scientists, astronauts and aliens, and filmed as *The Forbidden Planet* (1956), or that Aldous Huxley used *Brave New World* as the title for his dystopian novel (1932). *The Tempest* is not just Shakespeare's travel play, but his pioneering work of science fiction.

No less striking is the play's artfulness, the illusions, enchantments and mysterious symmetries that wrap around its characters. Not only is it haunted by 'noises' and 'sweet airs' (III.2.136–7), its music is more insistent and integral to the action than in any other Shakespearian drama. Music is constantly present (the only scenes not to call for it explicitly are I.1 and III.1), and its effects are complex and startling. It is used to charm and celebrate, but also to terrify, intimidate and compel. Music brings out suppressed desires in the characters' minds, provoking them to feelings of both yearning and despair. Caliban's dream, which tantalizes him with riches and leaves him weeping when they vanish at his awakening (III.2.140–44), encapsulates this mood of frustrated longing. The culmination of this strain is the miniature masque which the spirits perform in Act IV, until Prospero breaks its spell. Masques were courtly festivals of high sophistication, combining acting, song, dance, mythological themes and gorgeous costumes and scenery. Though he lives at the edge of Europe, Prospero conjures up a show redolent of the most expensive pleasures seen in any Italian court, albeit one which, as in all the masques performed at the Jacobean court, proves as evanescent as it is glorious. Anything seems possible on the island, whether it is phantom storms, invisible music, nymphs, harpies, vanishing banquets, flying goddesses, spirit dogs or dancing country-folk. What brings them into being is the technical wizardry of Shakespeare's playhouse, which is more apparent here than in any other play. *The Tempest* is the drama in which Shakespeare most fully exploits the magic of theatre.

Yet Shakespeare subjects this fantastic world to surprisingly realistic scrutiny, counterpointing the extraordinary with attitudes that are more disenchanted. That island experience which for Gonzalo and Miranda is a source of wonder is for Stephano and Sebastian an opportunity for political insurrection, and for Trinculo and Antonio – both of whom see Caliban as a 'strange fish' that may be 'marketable' at home (II.2.27, V.1.266) – potential good business. Even Prospero, whose magic invests him with control over life and death, has his power hedged around with a sense of its dangers and risks. He has to reconcile his righteous anger with pity for fellow human beings, and what could have been a moment of pure triumph over his enemies will be coloured by disappointment and regret. So for all its magic and wonders, the play will conclude with enchantments broken and a return to the difficult business of ordinary life. One irony of Miranda's 'brave new world' is that such an apostrophe would normally be directed by travellers to the exotic sights they had discovered, not be applied to the travellers themselves. What you take to be wonderful turns out to depend on where you stand to look at it.

In the genesis of the play, fact and fiction are difficult to disentangle. One possible point of origin can be traced to events that took place two years before Shakespeare wrote (the earliest reference to *The Tempest* is a record of performance at court in November 1611). In the summer of 1609 an expedition to Virginia, led by Sir Thomas Gates and Sir George Somers, ran into trouble in mid-Atlantic. Gates and Somers had been commissioned to take charge of the English colony at Jamestown (established in 1607, and already struggling to survive), but while trying to pick up the trade winds their ship was overtaken by a hurricane and carried hundreds of miles off course. This violent storm lasted for four days, during which time the ship leaked badly and passengers and crew together laboured ceaselessly to save her. 'The storm in a restless tumult' (wrote William Strachey, one of the gentlemen travelling with Gates)

had blown so exceedingly as we could not apprehend in our imaginations any possibility of greater violence, yet did we still find it not only more terrible but more constant, fury added to fury, and one storm urging a second more outrageous than the former ... Our sails wound up lay without their use, and ... six and sometimes eight men were not enough to hold the whipstaff [tiller] in the steerage ... It could not be said to rain, the waters like whole rivers did flood in the air ... During all this time the heavens looked so black upon us that it was not possible the elevation of the pole might be observed; nor a star by night nor sunbeam by day was to be seen.

Eventually the ship ran aground in the Bermudas, an uninhabited archipelago of bad reputation known to sailors as the Devil's Islands, but which turned out to be surprisingly hospitable. 'It pleased our merciful God' (wrote a much relieved Strachey) 'to make even this hideous and hated place both the place of our safety and means of our deliverance.' Here the crew harvested fruits, berries, fish, fowl, pigs and turtles, and survived for ten months until they had built new ships and could sail on to Virginia. Unfortunately they found the colony in desperate straits, and Strachey's story continues with rebellion and disorder amongst the settlers, to which Gates responded rather like Prospero, with violent punishments and the imposition of a draconian penal code.

Strachey's vivid eyewitness narrative, *A True Reportory of the Wrack and Redemption of Sir Thomas Gates*, was not printed until 1625, but the story of the voyagers' loss and miraculous recovery became a hot topic in the summer of 1610, when the news trickled back to England. Probably Shakespeare read Strachey's report in manuscript, and other shorter accounts were also published. It is true that its verbal similarities with the play are only passing and tentative, and the play does not contain anything that Shakespeare could not have invented without it. He already knew about 'hurricanoes' when he wrote *King Lear* (see *King Lear*, III.2.2). However, Ariel's claim that he presented himself in flames on the mast and rigging (I.2.198–201) recalls Strachey's astonished description of the electrical phenomenon known as St Elmo's fire, and his reference to Prospero sending him to fetch dew from the 'still-vexed Bermudas' (I.2.229) points strongly towards the Atlantic. It would have been hard for the first audiences to see *The Tempest* without

thinking of the savage storm and seemingly providential
redemption which had been common talk just months
before.

The presence of this material in the play helps to
explain its slightly confusing geography. Although the
island is located in the Mediterranean, it carries traces of
the New World which suggest that Shakespeare's imagination was ranging more globally – the most striking
example being Miranda's famous phrase with which this
introduction began. Caliban tells us that his mother
worshipped a god called Setebos (I.2.373, V.1.261), but
this was a name from South America, which Shakespeare
found in narratives of discovery in Patagonia. Gonzalo's
fantasy of a utopian state (II.1.144–64) is developed from
an essay by the French philosopher Michel de Montaigne,
'Of the Cannibals', discussing the discovery of new races
across the Atlantic, and he talks about making 'plantation' of the island, by which he means 'settlement'.
Gonzalo is not himself a colonist – nor, indeed, is the
island unsettled – but this was the vocabulary used of
American enterprise and colonization rather than
Mediterranean commerce. Trinculo's plan to take Caliban
home and exhibit him for money recalls the many New
World natives who were brought back to Europe as
strange sights from the mid sixteenth century onwards.
And the presentation of Caliban as a slave resonates even
more strongly with the Americas. The transportation of
black African slaves to Spanish and Portuguese colonies
in Brazil, Mexico and the Caribbean was already an
established trade, and it would in time become indelibly
associated with North America.

It is probably too much to claim, as some readers have
done, that *The Tempest* is Shakespeare's American play,
or that Caliban's song 'Freedom, high-day! High-day,

freedom!' (II.2.185) is the first American poem. To do so is to move the island too far westward, and ignore its ties with the North African coast and the affairs of old Europe, which are just as strong. Prospero and the other Italians are intent on getting to Naples, not Virginia. Still, Shakespeare must have been deeply read in the literature of exploration (such as the collections of travel stories compiled by Richard Eden and Richard Hakluyt), and his depiction of Prospero as a severe master to his servants raises associations with the colonial past which (as we shall see) in modern times have proved impossible to overlook. Moreover, the play has become part of the contemporary literature of colonialism, for many twentieth-century poets, novelists and polemicists have 'written back' to it, reading modern colonial relations through the matrix of Prospero's treatment of Caliban, or giving Caliban and his mother Sycorax voices which allow them to articulate the point of view of the aboriginal races who in this period were becoming the objects of European discovery. For example, in *The Pleasures of Exile* (1960), the black Barbadian novelist George Lamming reflects on Caliban as a way of exploring feelings of alienation bred by his own position as the descendant of slaves, and in *Prospero and Caliban* (1964) the French social scientist Octave Mannoni took the main characters as symbols for what he thought was the psychology of colonialism he had observed in Madagascar. In *Highlife for Caliban* (1995), the Sierra Leonean poet Lemuel Johnson imagines Caliban as king in his own kingdom, and Sycorax is the central character of Marina Warner's novel *Indigo* (1992), transformed into a native woman on the fictitious West Indian island of Enfant-Béate whose life is tragically altered by the arrival of English settlers. And there are literally scores of other examples, from Africa, South America, the Caribbean, Australia, New Zealand. No other play, not even *Hamlet*, has had such a vigorous and controversial afterlife. Part of its continuing power is its ability to re-verberate with imperial themes, even if, as in many of these examples, modern writers typically seek to challenge the story, identifying blind spots, revising its politics or opening it out to counter-readings that cut across the grain. Although *The Tempest* does not have to be a colonial play, these resonances have ensured that it remains a living text for contemporary culture.

Of course, this is not the first storm in Shakespeare, nor would Shakespeare have needed to be moved by 'real' events in order to devise one. Irrespective of what had recently been happening on the high seas, the cataclysmic shipwreck is a recurrent motif in romance literature. By beginning with a tempest in which families are sundered and fortune does its worst, Shakespeare was tracking back to territory which he had begun to explore in his early comedies. Already in *The Comedy of Errors* there is a family which is separated by shipwreck twenty years before the action starts and which regroups in circum-stances of great coincidence, and in *Twelfth Night* the love affairs of Viola, Olivia and Orsino are bracketed by the sea-storm that casts Viola up in one place and her brother not too far away on the same coast, from where they will eventually reunite. Both of these shipwrecks happen in the Mediterranean. The device of separation and reunion which these comedies use as a structural frame was borrowed from the prose romances of Shakespeare's day, in which such motifs were common-place. Elizabethan romances (and their many precursors in classical literature from the first century AD onward) were early forerunners of the novel, with plots that typically depict ordinary people undergoing extraordinary sufferings or engaged in long, hazardous and seemingly haphazard travels. The life-changing storm had a literary prehistory long before William Strachey's adventures.

The seminal Elizabethan romance, Sir Philip Sidney's *Arcadia* (1580/93), begins with a shipwreck in which its heroes are cast adrift. Their helplessness before winds and waters suggests the fragility of their lives and the inability of even the most determined persons to control their own destiny. In Virgil's Latin epic *The Aeneid* – not a romance, but related to the form – the hero Aeneas, whose destiny is to found the Roman empire, is knocked off course by a storm at the very start. He comes to shore at Carthage, which, interestingly, is virtually the same geographical spot that Shakespeare's Alonso has sailed from (and *The Tempest* pointedly echoes *The Aeneid* in several places: see the notes to I.2.421, II.1.77, 80, 113–22, III.3 headnote and IV.1.102). Other disasters that strike in such literature include kidnapping by brigands, slavery, rape and apparent death through poison or drugs. Yet after great suffering, sometimes extending over a period of years, the characters of romance at last accidentally drift together again and are reunited in scenes of almost unbearable joy, in which that which was thought to be lost is surprisingly recovered. The whole concluding movement of *The Tempest* is a sustained 'recognition scene' of this kind. Alonso reacts to the return of Ferdinand as if he had been lost for years, not just a few hours.

In his later plays, Shakespeare was repeatedly drawn to romance plots. *Pericles*, *Cymbeline* and *The Winter's Tale* all feature stories in which families are split apart by chance, error or bad fortune, and after much suffering are reunited; both *Pericles* and *The Winter's Tale* use ship-wrecks as agents of this separation. In such plots, there is always a strong magnetic force at work to ensure that the future will turn out happily. Often it feels as if some invisible hand is influencing events, like the goddess Diana in *Pericles*, Jupiter in *Cymbeline* or Apollo in *The Winter's Tale*, guaranteeing that at some indeterminate point the characters' sorrows will end. This ensures that romance structures are powerfully end-stopped and culminate in a mood of raptness expressing the characters' relief at finding their lives unexpectedly redeemed. A hidden controlling pattern is suddenly revealed beneath the random events, creating new prospects that transform their former sufferings. Like Alonso, whose drowned body is imagined turning into coral and pearls, they 'suffer a sea-change | Into something rich and strange' (I.2.400–401).

Yet the form is not exactly optimistic, for there is often something arbitrary about romance reunions. The characters have not brought about their own happiness, nor is it always clear why they should be rewarded, or why the rewards should come at this particular moment. Romance thus underlines the individual's insignificance and vulnerability, even as it provides a structure within which families find their lives falling into place. Why should Prospero have this chance, which mysteriously depends on an 'auspicious star' (I.2.182)? So too romance theology remains agnostic, even though its conclusions seem miraculous. The pattern is not a moral scheme that punishes shortcomings and rewards virtue; the characters suffer simply because loss, separation and hardship are the common lot of everyone. And there may also be some shortfall in the ending, some pain which has not been wiped away (like the dead child Mamillius in *The*

Winter's Tale, who cannot be made to return). In *The Tempest*, the vein of scepticism that countervails the closing mood is unusually insistent. Gonzalo voices the note of wonder – 'O, rejoice | Beyond a common joy, and set it down | With gold on lasting pillars' (V.1.206–8) – but he is the play's most idealistic character, who always looks for the silver lining. The audience may be more aware of the cynics Antonio and Sebastian, who stay outside the charmed circle, or of Caliban's troubling presence, or of Prospero's attitude of inner distance from the celebrations that he has nonetheless engineered. Nor are we allowed to forget that, with Prospero pulling the strings, everything that Gonzalo takes for miraculous has at some level been theatrically contrived.

The Tempest is unusual in compressing the romance form so radically. Most romances are ramshackle structures that sprawl across time and space in imitation of their characters' travels (the action of *The Winter's Tale* takes sixteen years, *Cymbeline* ranges from Britain to Italy). Shakespeare takes this rambling, episodic mode and gives it unprecedented focus, confining its action to a single place and to one day. Indeed, the events appear to occupy real time, needing no more space than the three hours that the performance requires in the theatre. This technically brilliant imitation of the neoclassical unities (which laid down that plays should be confined to a single day and location) runs counter to Shakespeare's customary practice, for he is often quite cavalier with time and place, and is particularly counter-intuitive for romance, a form which normally depends on amplitude and the almost endless deferral of resolution. Instead of following events over their temporal and physical sweep, Shakespeare gives us only the moment of culmination. The vast romance perspectives are brought to bear internally, through the action of memory, the 'dark backward and abysm of time' (I.2.50) where the play's prehistory has slowly accumulated. The past is thus telescoped into the present through men's ability to remember, with Prospero's scheme to recover his power a kind of Freudian shock, bringing people face to face with memories that they had tried to repress. This arrangement motivates the long second scene, with its narratives of Prospero's, Ariel's and Caliban's past histories, each nested intricately inside one another, and it produces the harpy's stunning rebuke to Alonso, forcing him to dredge up recollections about his seizure of power over which he is in denial: 'remember – | For that's my business to you' (III.3.68–9). Memory is indeed the play's business. It is the trap in which Prospero's enemies are caught, by which they stand accused and which they must discharge by making reparation. The one thing they cannot escape is their past.

Prospero's obsession with the past makes him the play's dominant figure. In Peter Greenaway's film adaptation, *Prospero's Books* (1991), Sir John Gielgud speaks not only Prospero's lines but those of all the other characters, and this makes it seem as if the whole movie is a talking therapy going on inside Prospero's head. But Prospero is also dominant because of the control permitted by his magic, which draws attention to the contrivances involved in the plot. As we shall see, Prospero's magic raises questions about his intentions and power, but what it particularly does to the play's design is prevent us from taking anything for the reality that it purports to be. The double vision that it creates is evident from the spectacularly deceitful opening. The storm scene does all it can to promote an impression of realism. No other play begins with quite such a *coup de théâtre*, plunging us without

preparation into violent action which is at once pitiful
and terrifying. The emphasis is on authenticity and believ-
ability. Shakespeare ransacked the glossaries of seamanship to ensure that his sailors spoke the language of
nautical life and that the events seemed technically
convincing. Yet within an instant – like a court masque
in which a scene of thunderous tempest is brushed aside
to reveal a serene landscape – the weather clears and it
becomes evident that all this menace has been merely an
illusion. In some productions directors bring Ariel or
Prospero onstage to oversee the storm, but this device
gives the game away at the outset. Shakespeare's strategy
is to wrong-foot the audience and allow them an unsettling initial taste of Prospero's power. After this
opening, in which apparently tragic circumstances turn
out to be a magician's charm, we can never be quite sure
where reality ends and theatre begins. It makes the whole
play provisional, an act of imaginative collusion, in which
whatever resolutions are achieved will always be understood on one level as effects of art.

Until comparatively recent times, Prospero was regarded
as a benign patriarch, whose influence over the lives of
his fellows was entirely admirable. Most productions and
criticism down to the mid twentieth century treated him
as a prickly but essentially lovable figure, whose actions
were motivated by care for his daughter, duty to his state,
and righteous anger against his enemies (for some fuller
details, see The Play in Performance). But these days
Prospero has started to seem less benevolent. On modern
stages he often appears tetchy, irascible and self-doubting,
and his influence over the other characters' lives
frequently appears controlling rather than reassuring.
His relationships with his family have acquired overtones

of suspicion, strain and paranoia, and the restraint of his own anger sometimes seems hard-won. The play itself gives us surprisingly little guidance about these things. For all his detailed narration of his past fortunes, Prospero remains opaque, his motives and intentions difficult to fathom. Had he always planned to forgive his enemies, or is his affirmation that the 'rarer action is | In virtue than in vengeance' (V.1.27–8) something that comes to him only as an afterthought? Does he want Ferdinand to have Miranda, or does his pretence of violence towards his future son-in-law express some hidden jealousy? Does he mean to take some sort of responsibility for what Caliban has become when he says 'this thing of darkness I | Acknowledge mine' (275–6)? Partly the uncertainty is created because the text gives him scarcely any soliloquies in which he might express himself privately, and allows him to be played with equal plausibility as kindly father-figure, troubled sufferer or resentful autocrat. In the twentieth century, though, the darker options have been increasingly preferred.

To a considerable degree this change reflects long-term historical shifts which have undermined the moral and political assumptions on which the story rests, and have driven a wedge between our expectations and those of Shakespeare's audience, particularly over the proper ordering of the family and the state. In Shakespeare's day, the idea that a king ought to be a kind of father to the state, and that a father was a kind of ruler within his own domestic kingdom, was deeply ingrained – or at least it was widely spoken of as a possible and effective model for government in both public and private life. It is certainly the way that James I saw himself, whether or not we consider this to be something that Shakespeare was likely to endorse. The idea of a state run by a single ruler answerable only to God is not, on the whole, appealing to modern spectators, while ideas about parenting have moved a long way from Prospero's authoritarian mode. Nor do modern audiences have quite so much anxiety as does Prospero about the dangers of masterlessness, the requirement that all members of the state should be obedient and acknowledge the rule of their overlord – an issue which is announced in the opening scene, when Antonio arrives on deck asking 'Where's the Master?' and gets the reply 'What cares these roarers for the name of king?' (I.i.9, 16–17. The waves are meant, but 'roarers' was a word used idiomatically at this time to mean riotous and disorderly people, as in the expression 'roaring boys'.) Of course, Shakespeare does not make Prospero immune from criticism and puts his claims to political and domestic authority under intense scrutiny. Still, if today we are uncomfortable with the authoritarian cast of Prospero's fatherhood, it signals that on some level we are struggling with the historical distance between what was expected from a ruler in Shakespeare's time and our own.

Prospero's story will always be a personal odyssey, involving patience rewarded, suffering overcome and reconciliation – of a sort – working through. The struggle between revenge and forgiveness is the central dynamic of his role. But it is difficult to overlook the politics that condition his behaviour, given that he is a duke as well as a father. His choices regarding his family are intricately bound up with his position as former Duke of Milan, so that everything he does in the home has a pay-off for the political power that he hopes to recover. It is very striking that the dynastic story involving the affairs of Milan and Naples and the family crisis go hand in hand, the two aspects being so closely knit that they cannot be disentangled. Prospero begins the play under threat in both the family and the state. His position is weak because he is an elder brother who has been displaced by his younger sibling, and because he is a father who, in the absence of male heirs, has no effective future. At the same time, as Duke of Milan, his small but independent territory has been brought into fealty to the much larger kingdom of Naples. His plan to assert power in the family has everything to do with recouping power in Milan.

In presenting events in Milan, Shakespeare deliberately leaves the circumstances of Prospero's exile ambiguous. Prospero was clearly betrayed by his enemies, but it is also implied that he contributed to his downfall by forgetting his responsibilities: 'all dedicated | To closeness and the bettering of my mind', he 'neglect[ed] worldly ends', thinking instead that his 'library | Was dukedom large enough' (I.2.89–90, 109–10). So his exile is partly a consequence of his ineffectiveness as a ruler, which prevents us from taking absolutely for granted his assumption that he has an inherent right to govern. However, the emotional charge associated with the exile derives from the element of family treachery, in that Prospero has been displaced by his younger brother. In a society based on the principle of primogeniture this reverses the usual hierarchy. The custom would be for the first son to inherit property and power and for his brother to make his own way in the world, so in trying to reclaim his inheritance Prospero is reasserting what in legal terms would be the proper order of things. This is what makes his demand to Antonio – '[I] require | My dukedom of thee, which perforce I know | Thou must restore' (V.1.132–4) – feel like a return to both domestic and political normality (though Shakespeare had earlier treated the plight of younger brothers more sympathetically in *As You Like It*). Moreover, Antonio has compounded the offence by leaguing with Alonso, so that the dukedom of Milan loses its independence by being drawn into the political orbit of a more powerful state. Prospero's response is to outflank his usurping brother by forging a connection with Alonso based on dynastic marriage rather than political alliance.

The beauty of this plan is that it solves the other problem that Prospero has, the absence of male progeny. In this regard, he is like many other Shakespearian rulers whose situation is unstable because they cannot securely pass their power on to the next generation. Like Leontes in *The Winter's Tale* (who loses his son Mamillius), Pericles (who has only a daughter), Cymbeline (who is unaware that his two missing sons are alive), and even King Lear (who has three daughters but no son and so conceives his disastrous plan to divide the inheritance between them), Prospero's authority is weakened by his lack of a male heir. However powerful he is in the present, some future point must come at which his rule is handed on, but the failure of biological provision makes dynastic continuity uncertain. Power is likely to flow out of the dynasty, or (in family terms) the father will be reduced to the status of a mere father-in-law. These circumstances put special pressure on his relationship with Miranda, since she is effectively the channel through which his authority will be transmitted into the future. Prospero spends much of the play making arrangements for Miranda's marriage, singling out Ferdinand from the rest of the courtiers, encouraging the two to fall in love and staging what is effectively a betrothal ceremony in the masque. When the Neapolitan court reassembles, Alonso is presented with a fait accompli: he has a new daughter-in-law, and one who offers a political connection guaranteeing that Prospero will be restored to his dukedom. Yet of course this is only a partial triumph, since even this stratagem cannot preserve Prospero's long-term control of his state. He is returned to rule, but at his death the inheritance will pass to Ferdinand, and in the next generation Milan will become a possession of Naples. Even as Prospero resumes his power, he loses it. There is no way that he can protect Milanese independence beyond his lifetime.

What of Miranda's part in all of this? It is important that she be seen to fall in love with Ferdinand, that she is a willing wife and he a deserving husband. The sequence in which he is put to work carrying logs is a device to validate him by displaying his chivalric side. A pointless task such as knights are forced to do in romance as a test of worthiness, the log-carrying is taken by Ferdinand as an opportunity to show his devotion to his mistress. It fills out his character by displaying his lack of snobbery and prudishness, and proves that he understands that Miranda is a prize to be earned, not stolen or seized as if of right. His sentimental education – 'Some kinds of baseness | Are nobly undergone, and most poor matters | Point to rich ends' (III.1.2–4) – demonstrates that he deserves to have her. For her part, Miranda, who has spent her entire life under her father's control, suddenly discovers a yearning for another man, and embarks in a quiet but determined way on one of the play's many rebellions. Prospero is pleased to see her falling for Ferdinand, but it is still a kind of revolt, for to help him she must disobey her father's commands, and her avowal of love is made with heroic finality: 'I am your wife, if you will marry me; | If not, I'll die your maid' (83–4). She is crossing a life threshold, and although she does what Prospero would have her do, he is at the same time losing her to someone else. Again, he forfeits something, even as he gets what he wants.

Still, Miranda's happiness is not the only issue, since on another level Prospero's preoccupation with her marriage is coloured by political considerations. As daughter to a duke, she is the dynastic cement through which Milan and Naples must be bound together. Prospero tells her that all his plans are conceived 'in care of thee – | Of thee, my dear one, thee my daughter' (I.2.16–17), and this is clearly true, but everything depends on her falling in love with Ferdinand and willingly opting for the marriage which Prospero intends. To modern ears, attuned as we are to notions of free choice in love, Miranda's situation may sound constrained, though it is a consequence of her position as an heiress rather than anything peculiar to Prospero's family. In all princely or aristocratic households at this time, the marriage of the daughter was as much a property transaction as an affair of the heart. Daughters carried with them part of the family's estate, honour and identity, so their espousals were matters of intense interest and anxiety. For example, in the England of 1611, everyone would have been well aware that something would soon have to be done for James I's daughter, Princess Elizabeth, who was nearly of marriageable age. In 1613 she would be wedded to the Prince Elector Frederick V, after the briefest of courtships, and sent into Germany, never to see her family again. One of the plays performed at court for the marriage celebrations was *The Tempest*.

If anything, Prospero is unusual for the tenderness he shows Miranda, the sensitivity with which he handles her predicament. Nevertheless, the play makes it apparent that her marriage is designed, since he engineers it. He arranges for the couple to meet, eavesdrops on their seemingly private talk in Act III, scene 1, and gives Miranda to Ferdinand as a 'gift' or 'compensation' (IV.1.2, 8) for his sufferings. The marriage is a love match, but that makes it no less an arrangement between father and son-in-law. It is not clear what would have happened had Miranda not fallen in love with Ferdinand, and while she goes happily to Naples, the play hints that, in life off the island, happy ever after cannot be guaranteed. There is the merest touch of irony in the final scene when, at the moment that Miranda and Ferdinand are discovered playing chess, she is complaining that he has cheated: 'Sweet lord, you play me false' (V.1.172). Whatever the future holds, this is no naive romance.

Rather more problematic is the case of Claribel, daughter to Alonso, whose marriage to the King of Tunis is not voluntary. Sebastian complains to Alonso about this choice:

> You were kneeled to and importuned otherwise
> By all of us, and the fair soul herself
> Weighed between loathness and obedience at
> Which end o'th'beam should bow. (II.1.128–31)

Claribel's unhappy marriage across boundaries of race is a disenchanted version of the union between dynasties that Miranda facilitates, presenting in a more extreme form the differences which it was the woman's job to bridge. Miranda unites rival families and states, but for Claribel the requirement that the woman reconcile opposites and marry beyond the horizons of the family is traumatic. A reluctant Desdemona, last heard of 'Ten leagues beyond man's life' (246), Claribel is one of the casualties that haunt the play. A shadow of Miranda, whose future will not be put right no matter what happens in Italy, she signals an inequality that Prospero's magic takes for granted. Europe's domestic and political arrangements depend on the compliance of its women.

The other side of this question is the way that Prospero's success is bound up with control of Miranda's chastity. Prospero is surprisingly obsessed with the lovers' sexual continence. Miranda is well aware that she is undergoing a sexual awakening – hence her barely coded remarks to Ferdinand about 'What I desire to give' and 'What I shall die to want' (III.1.78–9) – but Prospero is insistent that desire must be restrained within the bounds of marriage. He is highly suspicious of Ferdinand's intentions, and imposes the log-carrying on him out of anxiety that he may not love her enough: 'this swift business | I must uneasy make, lest too light winning | Make the prize light' (I.2.450–52). By setting him to the same labour that he had earlier imposed on Caliban, Prospero implies that the two characters are reflections of one another, and need similar chastening. Later, giving Miranda away, he sternly warns Ferdinand about waiting for the wedding night:

> If thou dost break her virgin-knot before
> All sanctimonious ceremonies may
> With full and holy rite be ministered,
> No sweet aspersion shall the heavens let fall
> To make this contract grow; but barren hate,
> Sour-eyed disdain and discord shall bestrew
> The union of your bed with weeds so loathly
> That you shall hate it both. (IV.1.15–22)

Ferdinand gives the requisite assurances, but Prospero returns to the topic moments later (51–4), and the theme of the masque that follows, marking their betrothal, is the need to police extramarital desire.

The masque is a celebration of fertility. Ceres, the goddess of harvest, and Juno, the goddess of childbirth, are called down by Iris, the goddess of peace, to bless this union, which they do in songs promising future abundance. Their language is densely larded with unusual words resonant of fruitfulness: 'rich leas', 'vetches', 'turfy mountains', 'meads thatched with stover', 'spongy April', 'bosky acres', 'foison plenty', 'sedged crowns' (IV.1.60–65, 81, 110, 129). The effect is all the stronger for the play's linguistic restraint elsewhere. The goddesses command the naiads to leave their streams and join in country dance with the reapers, their steps symbolically playing out the erotic encounters of marriage. The naiads are 'temperate' (132) but the 'sicklemen' are 'sunburned' (134), thus guaranteeing that sufficient biological heat will be produced. So Ferdinand and Miranda's marriage is predicted to be fertile, the perfect union of hot and cold, but the masque is equally insistent on denying access to the festivities to Venus and Cupid. These are, of course, the goddess of love and her son, whose presence we might expect at a wedding, but here they are invoked as patrons of unruly lust and merely physical desire. Venus – 'Mars's hot minion' (98) – and 'waspish-headed' Cupid (99), we are told, had hoped to do some 'wanton charm' (95) on the lovers, but the couple have vowed to abstain from sex until 'Hymen's torch be lighted' (97) – that is, until their marriage has been solemnized (Hymen being the god of marriage). The masque thus drives home the point that while sexual activity between the lovers will be pleasurable, it must be directed towards the producing of children and is legitimate only when temperate and only within the institutional context of marriage. This is precisely the promise that Ferdinand has already made (23–31).

As with Prospero's obsession with Miranda's marriage, his investment in her chastity is not unusual. For all Renaissance princes, the woman's sexual purity was necessary for dynastic honour and the safe transfer of inheritance. The father had to be sure that his children were indeed his own, and there are more remarks on this theme – some rather off-colour – about Prospero's wife and his mother, both long-dead (I.2.56–9, 117–20). Since Miranda is moving from the state of daughter to that of wife, she is in a transitional or 'liminal' phase where the lines of loyalty are muddled up, and this inevitably attracts anxiety. Authority cannot be safely passed from father to son-in-law unless care is taken to ensure the woman's obedience. We need only recall Brabantio's difficulties with Desdemona in *Othello* to see how fraught such transitions could be. Moreover, this is not the first time that Prospero has worried about Miranda's virginity, for the main accusation that he lays against Caliban is that he tried 'to violate | The honour of my child' (347–8). Caliban does not bother to deny this, and one can see why Prospero should be upset, but – without wishing to condone Caliban or make light of his crime – it is symptomatic that it should be an attempt to rape Miranda that provokes Prospero to treat him so harshly. A deflowered daughter would have tainted the family, and Caliban speaks of the attempted rape in terms which draw out its implied political challenge to her father: 'O ho, O ho! Would't had been done! | Thou didst prevent me. I had peopled else | This isle with Calibans' (349–51). Caliban fantasizes not about the physical pleasure of the act but the power it would have brought, creating for him a dynasty – indeed, a race –

over which he might have ruled. King Caliban's imagined family uncannily echoes the circumstances of Duke
Prospero's household, and the pleasure he would have
taken in fatherhood is an unsettling, if distorted, mirror
of Prospero's image of his own authority. The only
thing that makes Caliban containable is the fact that he
has no partner and hence (as yet) no children. If for
Prospero his daughter's progeny is the hope that redeems
his power, the corollary is that Caliban must not be
allowed to breed at all.

All of which has brought us to Caliban. Having at one
time been regarded as little more than an amusing fantasy
figure, he has in the modern era often been taken for the
centre of the play, in spite of the fact that he speaks barely
170 lines. His distinctive characteristic is his lack of
distinctive characteristics. He is spoken of as, variously,
a slave, 'freckled whelp' (I.2.283), beast, fish, devil, demi-
devil, tortoise, 'mooncalf' and 'puppy-headed monster'
(II.2.111, 154–5). There is little in the language to tell us
what he really looks like, though Prospero's remark that
Caliban was once the only 'human shape' on the island
(I.2.284) and Miranda's that Ferdinand is the third man
she has seen (444–5) do establish that he is at least
humanoid. His mother was certainly human, a woman
from Algiers in north Africa, though she too carries the
taint of monstrosity by her association with witchcraft
and her physical deformity – bowed into a hoop through
'age and envy' (258) – and his father is not known, though
Prospero thinks it was the devil himself (319). Onstage
Caliban has constantly changed: he has been a monkey,
a hairy wild man, a noble savage, even the missing link.
He attracts notice because we never know quite what he
is and he evades categorization, allowing everyone to

project onto him their sense of what they find 'monstrous' or 'other'. A theatrical black hole, he is defined not by his own identity but by what others see in him or make of him. Errant child, rebellious servant, malicious rapist, oppressed slave, he can be recruited to many different perspectives, though the common thread is always the same, that what we feel about him necessarily depends on what we feel about Prospero.

These days the almost inevitable association is with the tales of slavery, violence and expropriation that were so much part of the literature of discovery. The risk of emphasizing such links is that they narrow the possibilities for Caliban, writing out of the picture those elements which do not fit the colonial plot. Particularly, his ambiguous status as monster rather than man makes it impossible to sentimentalize him. He cannot easily be recruited to any colonial cause (at least, not without rewriting) because the text does not allow him to be straightforwardly human. The uncertainty over his identity means that he is always touched by qualities of the fantastic or grotesque. It is, though, difficult to avoid catching echoes in his story of the depressingly familiar scenario of gullible Indian and wily incomer, or treacherous native and betrayed settler. Caliban reminds Prospero of how in their early days 'Thou strok'st me, and made much of me', gave him 'Water with berries in't' (I.2.333–4) and taught him his words. In return for this friendship he showed him 'all the qualities o'th'isle' (337), only for Prospero to take over the island, set him under subjection and punish him for his failure to live as his new master would have him. For his part, Prospero recounts a history of treachery, viciousness and insubordination, in which his trust was rewarded with betrayal, and Caliban's servitude imposed as the inevitable consequence of his brutish nature, his inability to live by the codes which the European brought with him.

Between these two narratives it is hard to adjudicate. They are recognizably versions of the same events, though they are told from radically opposing perspectives. Prospero justifies his treatment of Caliban as a political necessity bred out of his ineducability, his resistance to European values. Caliban was treated as one of the family, but turned out to be 'A devil, a born devil, on whose nature | Nurture can never stick; on whom my pains, | Humanely taken, all, all lost, quite lost' (IV.1.188–90). Nurture having failed, Prospero resorts to force, for the chastity of Miranda has to be protected. Caliban's recalcitrant 'nature' thus necessitates the severity of Prospero's government. Being a 'monster', he has to be controlled. On the other side, there is some justice in Caliban's complaint that Prospero has violated his property rights, and the land ought to be his by right of prior possession: 'This island's mine, by Sycorax my mother, | Which thou tak'st from me' (I.2.331–2). What we think of these incompatible versions of the past will depend on how much credit we give to the speakers. It is striking that Prospero never actually denies Caliban's account of his inheritance, that the island once was his – though his attitude is implicit when he says Caliban was 'litter[ed]' here, like an animal, rather than born (282). Instead, Prospero bases his right to power on moral rather than territorial legitimacy. Caliban cannot rule the island because he is not really human, and cannot rule himself. But although Caliban may be a rapist, he is more complicated than the 'monster' Prospero takes him for. Shakespeare unsettles the situation by giving us Caliban's touchingly aesthetic response to the island's 'Sounds, and sweet airs' (III.2.137), which suggests he is not the simple

brute that the Europeans automatically assume. As
Coleridge said, 'Caliban is in some respects a noble
being: the poet has raised him far above contempt'
(*Shakespearean Criticism* (1960), II.138).

Having established Caliban's past history, Shakespeare
then plays it out a second time in the events involving
Trinculo and Stephano. Here Caliban repeats the cycle
of welcome and betrayal, though this time the rights and
wrongs are more clear-cut, and what earlier could have
been tragedy is replayed as farce. Stephano and Trinculo
are no high-minded promoters of civilization but small
men out for what they can get. Trinculo immediately
sizes up the 'strange fish' as a potential source of profit,
and Stephano has political ambitions, happy to be cast
up on an island where he can set up his own empire. They
introduce Caliban to something stronger than fruit-
flavoured mineral water, and he takes them for gods,
offering to show them the island just as he had done with
Prospero, then embarking on the plan to kill his master,
set up a new government and put Miranda in Stephano's
bed, brutally parodying Prospero's marriage plans for
Ferdinand (III.2.105–9). The irony here is that Caliban's
faith in Trinculo and Stephano, inspired by the bottle, is
completely misplaced. He sings his song of rebellion –
'Ban, ban, Ca-Caliban, | Has a new master, get a new
man! | Freedom, high-day! High-day, freedom! Freedom,
high-day, freedom!' (II.2.183–6) – but the prospects he
celebrates are not free at all. He has thrown off one master
in order to enslave himself to one even worse, and what
he takes for liberty is only another version of subjection
('I'll kiss thy foot. I'll swear myself thy subject', he tells
Stephano (152)). Emancipation is a long way off. Caliban
has been exploited, but in some respects he has willingly
become a slave and brought his subjection upon himself.

The problem of Caliban's position is that he is a unique specimen, yet has nothing to which he can lay claim as his own. Whatever history or culture he possesses has been supplied by his master, and in the codes of behaviour by which Prospero sets so much store he is already labelled as inferior or a rebel. Caliban is well aware of this, for he complains that the language which he uses to communicate was given to him by Prospero, and so it implicitly subjects him even as he speaks it. It is the speech of the master and allows him no place in which he is not already fixed as a slave: 'You taught me language, and my profit on't | Is, I know how to curse. The red plague rid you | For learning me your language!' (I.2.363–5). It is unclear whether Caliban had his own language before Prospero arrived. Miranda says that in his original state he would 'gabble like | A thing most brutish' (356–7). Perhaps this was a non-European tongue which she did not understand, though we cannot be sure. For his part, Caliban recognizes that Prospero's political power lies in this presumption of cultural superiority, the fact that he commands words, knowledge and technical skills which give him the ability to compel service, even though he is physically weaker than his servants. Caliban instructs Trinculo and Stephano that they must disarm Prospero of his magic books before they attack him, since what makes him invulnerable is the technological superiority that they confer:

> Remember
> First to possess his books, for without them
> He's but a sot as I am, nor hath not
> One spirit to command: they all do hate him
> As rootedly as I. Burn but his books. (III.2.92–6)

From Caliban's point of view, Prospero's rarified intellectual pursuits can readily be seen to have practical uses.
His magic allows him to impose his will in situations that
he could not otherwise control, and like the fruits of tech-
nological wizardry which early modern explorers took
with them around the globe – guns, maps, compasses,
Bibles – it gives him his political edge. But the advantage of his intellectual superiority is cultural as well as
political: it sets Prospero the representative of civilized
accomplishment against Caliban the burner of books.
Caliban cannot resist or even answer Prospero back
without testifying to the cultural superiority of his master.

In *Une Tempête* (1968), a radical rewriting of the play
by Aimé Césaire – the Martiniquan dramatist and founder
of the Négritude movement – the author adjusts the
balance of the play by inventing a culture and a history
for Caliban that explains his sense of grievance. The
slave speaks fragments of Swahili, communes with
the voices of the forest and worships his own gods.
This removes the effect of political hierarchy, instead
presenting the story as a conflict between two cultures
neither of which is intrinsically superior, the culture of
the incomer versus the culture of the native. But
Shakespeare's Caliban cannot claim anything like the
same cultural validation – quite the reverse, in fact, for
his parentage links him to an acutely negative cultural
stereotype, the Algerian witch Sycorax. Sycorax – another
of the play's various ghosts – is associated with diabol-
ical magic that looks like the antitype of Prospero's lofty
and philosophical enchantments. Her 'earthy and
abhorred commands' (I.2.273), her violence and malice,
her racial difference, and the fact that she wields power
as an independent woman, all make her seem the polar
opposite to Prospero, the bad magic that validates his

good. Where Prospero is the magician as careful father, Sycorax is the bad mother, the violent matriarch. Caliban is demonized by his parentage as well as by the ambiguity of his species.

Yet Sycorax's magic complicates our assessment of Prospero, for she stands behind him as a shadow, not merely an antitype. Even more than her son, her presence in the play is defined by the words of her enemies, who are keen to underline her contrariety to the values of their world. But as many critics have pointed out, Prospero's magic too has its violence and dangers. He feels it must eventually be relinquished, and when he does so, it is in words that pointedly hark back to the classical witch Medea, in Ovid's *Metamorphoses*. In this famous Latin poem, taught to every Elizabethan schoolboy, Medea, notorious for her atrocious crimes, utters a magical incantation which recounts the terrible deeds she has done, how she has raised storms, called down thunder, uprooted oaks, opened graves and let forth their dead. Shakespeare takes these unforgettable images and weaves them into Prospero's abjuration ('Ye elves of hills, brooks, standing lakes', etc. (V.1.33)), so that even as he abandons his 'rough magic' (50) he summons up the spectre of the archetypal witch whose power in some ways resembles his own. In particular, his claim to have raised the dead (made nowhere else in the play) invests him with the sorcerer's dangerous skill, necromancy. Sycorax is demonized by her association with Medea, whose appellation 'the Scythian raven' may be the etymological source of her name (see note to I.2.258), but something about Medea leaches into Prospero too. He is less the antithesis of Caliban than he would like us to think he is, and when he says 'this thing of darkness I | Acknowledge mine', he uses a language that signals paternity as much as ownership. It hints that, on some level, he too is parent to Caliban.

The other connection between Prospero and Sycorax is that both have Ariel for their servant. Prospero's releasing of Ariel from the cloven pine (I.2.291–3) reverses the violent magic which Sycorax had visited onto him, and his relationship with Ariel contributes to the many symmetries in this part of the play. He is the benevolent master to Sycorax's malicious tyrant, and Ariel is the servant whose grateful and willing obedience contrasts with the resentful Caliban. Caliban's claim that Prospero's spirits all 'hate him | As rootedly as I' (III.2.95–6) is not borne out by Ariel. Rather, the play stresses the delightfulness of Ariel's service, the way that Prospero's commands chime with aspects of his nature – the pleasure he takes in treading the ooze of the salt deep and running on the sharp wind of the north (I.2.252–4). Except when he manifests himself as a harpy or as Ceres, Ariel is unseen by anyone else, and this makes his symbiosis with Prospero appear uniquely intimate, the two of them inhabiting each other's space with almost telepathic intuition. 'Come with a thought', Prospero commands; 'Thy thoughts I cleave to' is the reply (IV.1.164–5). When Prospero leaves the island, the loss of Ariel's companionship will be another of the regrets that cloud his future, and nicknames like 'chick' and 'my tricksy spirit' (V.1.317, 226) only intensify the impression of interdependence. Indeed, Prospero is perhaps closer, certainly more open, to Ariel than to any of the human characters. As is shown by Ariel's advice to Prospero to be merciful rather than vindictive (17–24) – the only moment in the play when Prospero does what somebody else tells him – the spirit understands and appreciates him better than anyone. He is the other self that Miranda and Caliban can never quite be.

And yet we still register discordant notes in Ariel that allow Shakespeare to open the role to plural readings. Like everyone in the play, Ariel longs for freedom, and his service to Prospero is no less irksome for being pleasurable. He too is under an obligation and looks for a time when he will be his own master. He is capable of being 'Moody' (I.2.244), and this creates a space for tension which every production must acknowledge, at least to some degree. Very few will go so far as the 1993 Royal Shakespeare Company production, in which Simon Russell Beale's cool and fastidious Ariel hated his servitude and shocked Prospero by spitting in his face when he released him (a piece of stage business which the critics hated and which was abandoned early in the run). Still, all Ariels must have some desire to get away, which builds a discomfort into the role. No Prospero can entirely trust Ariel, for he will always be eager to depart, and Prospero only achieves his compliance by threatening to return him to the cloven pine from which he had released him. Inevitably, this threat draws attention to the ways in which Prospero's magic inhabits the space once occupied by that of Sycorax.

Of course, there is nothing personal in Ariel's moodiness, for he is defined by his freedom. It is his natural condition due to his lack of materiality as a spirit and is beautifully embodied in his songs: music is his very mode of being. Particularly, 'Where the bee sucks' (V.1.88) voices the life of unalloyed liberty into which he moves after the play ends, leaving him in a state of primal, undifferentiated pleasure. The irony of this is that it discloses how fettered all the human characters are, for even when they think themselves happy or free, they cannot escape the materiality of their existence. Ariel perhaps has the best claim of all to the island, yet he will

make nothing of it. The play is ambiguous about whether
Sycorax brought him to the island or whether he was
there when she arrived and was enslaved by her, but if
the latter scenario is correct, then in terms of priority the
island belongs to him, not Caliban. However, he is the
one figure who has no interest in owning it, or in owning
anything else. He alone can be free because he has no
needs, no possessions, no politics, no sexuality. When the
other characters feel the desires induced by Ariel's music,
they are yearning for a perfect liberty which, being
human, is the one thing that they can never know. For
us, freedom – at least, the kind into which Ariel mysteriously disappears at the end – will always be an unreal-
izable aspiration.

In their different ways, then, the stories of Miranda,
Caliban and Ariel play out the conditions of Prospero's
power. He is defined by his fatherhood, and if Miranda
is there to exhibit its domestic and dynastic implications,
Caliban and Ariel are necessary to give Prospero someone
to rule over. Without children or servants, Prospero
would have no authority. This is in striking contrast to
the vision of life on the island which Gonzalo conjures
up when he is trying to divert Alonso from his melancholy. In Act II, scene 1, Gonzalo imagines what this
apparently uninhabited island could be like under an ideal
ruler, and devises a recipe for perfect political freedom,
a Golden Age created from scratch:

> I'th'commonwealth I would by contraries
> Execute all things. For no kind of traffic
> Would I admit; no name of magistrate;
> Letters should not be known; riches, poverty,
> And use of service, none; contract, succession,

Bourn, bound of land, tilth, vineyard, none;
No use of metal, corn, or wine, or oil;
No occupation, all men idle, all;
And women too, but innocent and pure;
No sovereignty . . . (147–56)

The cynics, Sebastian and Antonio, poke fun at Gonzalo's fantasy, but his utopian ideas have a long intellectual prehistory, and adapt remarks from Montaigne's essay 'Of the Cannibals', which describes the challenge to European values posed by what was coming to be known about the American races and their way of life. Montaigne had met Indians transported into Europe from Brazil, and he was impressed by what seemed to be the unsophisticated freedoms that they enjoyed, the innocence of their life and the absence of many customs that made modern European society appear corrupt and decadent. Like Gonzalo, the encounter with a new world led him towards a radical critique of the values of his own society. The comparison between European civilization and the New World worked by no means to Europe's advantage.

   Gonzalo's ideas are attractive, but on many points the island commonwealth that Prospero has created reverses his emphases. Gonzalo would have no one labour on the island, but Prospero demands it. Indeed, he requires Ferdinand to carry logs like Caliban even though the task is pointless. Gonzalo's state would be free from contracts – that is, promises and legal bonds, what Sebastian glosses as 'No marrying 'mong his subjects' (II.1.165) – but Prospero imposes marriage and outlaws free love. In Gonzalo's primitivist Golden Age there would be no written literature or culture, but Prospero stages a masque and his books are the key to his power. And where Gonzalo would do away with sovereignty and the name of magistrate, Prospero's state turns centrally on sovereign authority. This is not to say that Prospero's civilization is right and Gonzalo's state of nature is wrong, for, as we have seen, the implications of Prospero's government are very thoroughly dissected. But the difference is that Gonzalo begins from the assumption that the islanders would be 'innocent and pure', whereas Prospero is a political pessimist, who assumes that men need to be ruled and that a state without a strong principle of kingly government will fall into a condition of anarchy.

As Sebastian and Antonio are quick to note (II.1.156–8), Gonzalo's utopia is self-contradictory, since he begins by supposing himself king of the isle, then denies that it will have any sovereignty. But Sebastian and Antonio's threat to Gonzalo is more urgent than nice points of literary criticism, since while the other courtiers sleep they conceive their plot to murder Alonso and usurp his power. This act of rebellion is another of the play's symmetries and repetitions, for the King of Naples' brother is persuaded to re-enact the political and domestic treason which had been performed against the Duke of Milan by his brother. The act which in the play's past was the cause of Prospero's exile looks like being repeated in the present against his enemy, and it suggests a different state of nature from that assumed in Gonzalo's utopia. Sebastian and Antonio are bad, ruthless men, who are not constrained by conscience or morality, and whose ethos is the law of the jungle or survival of the fittest. The only thing that has held Sebastian back from seizing power for himself is what he calls 'Hereditary sloth' (222), but in these unexpected circumstances Antonio urges him to seize his opportunity, and instructs him in the same arts of statecraft that Prospero remembers him as

having practised in Milan. There he had 'set all hearts
i'th'state | To what tune pleased his ear' (I.2.84–5) and
now he assures Sebastian that if he takes power Alonso's
followers will 'take suggestion as a cat laps milk'
(II.1.288). The only casualties will be his brother and
useless prating lords like Gonzalo who cannot be outfaced
since they place loyalty and morality above pragmatism
and realpolitik.

Alonso and Gonzalo are protected by Prospero, whose
magic ensures that the conspirators' plots cannot be
accomplished, but whether that magic has had any effect
on the minds of the perpetrators is a moot point. In the
final scene Antonio and Sebastian are allowed to return
home with Alonso, but there is little suggestion that their
behaviour off the island will be any different. Prospero
forgives Antonio, though in terms which suggest he does
it through gritted teeth – he cannot acknowledge him as
his brother, for example (V.1.130–32) – and neither
Antonio nor Sebastian offers any regrets. In fact, they
say nothing directly to Prospero at all. What keeps them
obedient is the simple fact of Prospero's knowledge of
their plans and his warning that he can expose them if
he wishes to do so: 'At this time | I will tell no tales'
(128–9). The loose threads left here allow the conclusion
to seem less than fully complete, and make it evident that
whatever the success of Prospero's strategy, his magic
has done little to make them better persons. He cannot
force his enemies to repent if they have no desire to do
so. Antonio and Sebastian are constrained by the threat
of exposure, the sword of Damocles that puts them on
their best behaviour, but only the most optimistic reading
can make it appear that they have really changed.

Prospero is more successful in making the other characters will the conclusion that he desires. The effect of

the harpy's visitation on Alonso – reminding him of his
seizure of power in Milan and blaming it for the loss of
his son – is to awaken his conscience, and throw him into
a trauma after which his rescue by Prospero comes like
a moment of soul-cleansing. The effect is all the more
impressive in that the harpy's terrifying words, warning
that the only escape is through 'heart's sorrow | And a
clear life ensuing' (III.3.81–2), are inaudible to the
courtiers who are free from guilt. When Alonso meets
Prospero, he at once resigns his dukedom and asks pardon
from him (V.1.111–19), then wishes that Miranda and
Ferdinand (whom as yet he thinks dead) could be alive
and ruling in Naples, which is just the solution that
Prospero wants to hear. The stings of conscience, then,
make Alonso subject himself to Prospero: the inner trajec-
tory which he follows gives meaning to Prospero's offer
of forgiveness. So too Caliban expresses regret in the
final moments, resolving to change and learn from his
mistakes: 'I'll be wise hereafter, | And seek for grace'
(295–6). Even Ferdinand and Miranda find that their love
makes them obedient and serviceable, for they enter into
a kind of bondage to each other that corresponds inwardly
to the physical labour that Ferdinand willingly performs.
Miranda offers herself to Ferdinand as his servant, and
he humbles himself to her, 'with a heart as willing | As
bondage e'er of freedom' (III.1.88–9), and takes Prospero
as a second father in place of Alonso (IV.1.123, V.1.195).
By the end of the play, almost all the characters have
moved into postures of obedience or alliance to Prospero.
The only exceptions are Antonio and Sebastian, whose
silence is the token of their imperfect assimilation.

     What puts the villains beyond Prospero's power is their
lack of conscience. Alonso and Caliban are capable of
being brought round because they can be made to feel

lx   *Introduction*

guilt and shame, but with Antonio and Sebastian such possibilities do not apply. Prospero pardons his brother, but the reconciliation, if that is the right word, is not unconditional. Although he forgives him, he still threatens to reveal the secret of his conspiracy and demands the return of his dukedom. His mercy is a device by which his brother can be kept under control, at least for now. Modern critics have felt some discomfort with this tactic, though it is clearly necessary since Antonio and Sebastian's propensity to violence (like Caliban's attempted rape) is a threat to their whole society. Without Prospero's surveillance the world would become a jungle. Still, Prospero has effectively engineered the conspiracy by using his magic to set up the opportunities that lead Antonio and Sebastian into it. He does this to bring them within the scope of his discipline, but it makes him more responsible for the criminals than he publicly admits, for he has provoked the crime in order that they will incur the punishment. In a court of law today – which *The Tempest* is not, of course – this might be regarded as entrapment. So too he exerts his hold over Alonso by keeping back until the last possible moment the information that his son has survived the shipwreck, and Caliban's rebellion seems no less a matter of his contriving. Stephano may sing 'Thought is free' (III.2.124), but with Ariel playing the tune the effect is ironic. However much Prospero is publicly committed to forgiveness, as a duke he must work by a more machiavellian rule-book. To Gonzalo it seems like a miracle, but Prospero knows that back in Milan miracles will not be enough. He returns to a world where the arts of power require an understanding of men's motives closer to that of his brother's. Perhaps this is one reason for the mood of regret that haunts him in the closing

moments, his perception of the gap between what his
magic purports to do and the reality.

Prospero's hesitation between revenge and forgiveness,
justice and mercy, severity and reconciliation, defines the
framework of the play. Whether events end triumphantly
or sourly will depend on the nature of his response to
Ariel's advice to be 'tender' towards his enemies. Deciding
that the 'rarer action is | In virtue than in vengeance'
(V.1.19, 27–8), Prospero opts to forgive, and the spare-
ness of the writing at this point allows actors to treat the
choice in many different ways. It can seem that Prospero
has always intended this, or that the change is sudden,
or is something which has gradually settled on him, or
which he is shamed into, or which he has no option but
to accept. But for all Prosperos, the price of forgiveness
is the requirement to forgo his magic. He cannot return
to the world of men if he continues to wield superhuman
power. Of course, Prospero no longer needs his charms,
for he already has everyone at his mercy, but there is a
strong tension in the play at this point, in that at the
moment when Prospero seems most in control of the
action, he has to forfeit everything that made him
powerful. He can return to everyday life only by setting
aside the thing that made him invulnerable and unique.
The emotional cost is expressed in the monologue that
follows ('Ye elves of hills, brooks, standing lakes'), which
celebrates but also separates him from his power. The
accomplishment of his plans coincides with a kind of
abdication, a moment of loss.
    In the latter part of the play, Prospero has seemed as
much aware of his power's ephemerality as of its dura-
bility. Although he stages a masque to celebrate his
daughter's dynastic marriage, instead of this courtly form

affirming the harmonies and prosperity of his state, it mysteriously collapses into discord, vanishing with a *'strange, hollow, and confused noise'* (IV.1.138). At Jacobean Whitehall, masques always led up to dancing between the courtiers and presented a great display of the opulence, confidence and majesty of kingly power. Prospero's masque ends differently, with the prince angry and 'distempered' (145), his family discomfited, the actors scattered and the festivity in disarray. The fantasy of endless bounty that the masque presents, of nature putting forth its abundance without limit or measure, recalls the Golden Age of Gonzalo's imagination, but it cannot be sustained. In the monologue 'Our revels now are ended' (148–58), spoken as a reaction to the masque's collapse, Prospero generalizes from the transformation scenes of court theatre to the impermanence of life. 'Revels' was the technical term for the social dancing on masque nights, and the 'vision' of towers, palaces and temples that he conjures alludes to Whitehall's scenic splendours, but here the emphasis is on their transience rather than glory. He dwells on the evanescence suggested by their changes of scenery and the morning-after effect that must often have been the experience of participants in these sometimes wearisome occasions. Such sentiments suggest Prospero's internal disenchantment with the mystique of his own sovereignty, the impossibility of ever drawing his state or family into the perfect harmony that the masque embodies. But his language also passes beyond reflections on the fragility of masque illusions into a larger doubt about existence itself, its briefness and lack of lasting value: 'We are such stuff | As dreams are made on, and our little life | Is rounded with a sleep.' The language of dreams and illusions has a melancholy wistfulness, but it is touched with suggestions of a nihilism to which, perhaps, idealists are constitutionally prone. Finding that life does not come up to the images that can be created by art, Prospero refuses to give it any more worth than a dream. The incompleteness of his masque measures the distance that he will have to travel on returning home.

Elsewhere in Shakespeare dreams are often profoundly meaningful, and for most of the characters the return to Milan will mark the start of a new life. Miranda is betrothed, the state is restored, Prospero, Alonso, even Caliban, have gone through changes of heart. The storm is a rite of passage that marks the traumas and mysterious renewals of change. They really have been alchemized into something 'rich and strange', reborn from the waters. The reunions of the final scene leave them in a state of breathless wonder, hardly daring to believe the miracles that seem to have come true. But in the Epilogue Prospero hangs back, putting himself for the last time at a distance from the other characters. His simple and direct language contrasts with the more heightened rhetoric that was used to voice the culminating discoveries, and he speaks not for the cast but in his own persona as actor, emphasizing the moment of disenchantment, the discarding of the role and the solitude into which he now falls. He ends in isolation, parted from his magic and from Miranda, Ariel and Caliban. Appealing ambiguously for forgiveness as well as applause, and emphasizing his helplessness and potential 'despair' (15), he returns us to the romance motif of the quest, the allegory of life as a journey towards fulfilment or judgement. But for Prospero the journey sounds tentative rather than confident, and his hope of becoming 'free' is expressed conditionally, dependent on the audience's willingness that he be 'pardoned' (19–20). Inevitably we clap and acknowledge the pleasure, surprise and imaginative bounty that the play has brought, but Prospero's intimation that 'Every third thought shall be my grave' (V.1.312) reminds us of what he is travelling towards, that for him this is the final journey. Going home will mean putting out the theatre lights for ever.

The Play in Performance

The Tempest is one of Shakespeare's shortest and most concentrated plays. There are only nine scenes, and, after the change of place at the end of Act I, scene 1, everything happens in the same location, the island. The three plots are bound tightly together by the presence of Prospero and Ariel as stage-managers or lookers-on, and Prospero further dominates because of his disproportionately large role (he has getting on for a third of the lines). The play involves surprisingly little action. Mostly the characters sit around and talk, remembering the past or planning for the future, and neither of the two conspiracies that threaten is allowed to come to anything. A recurrent motif is action interrupted or frustrated. There are, though, three big theatrical set-pieces – the storm, the vanishing banquet and the masque – which need careful handling, and the special atmosphere is intensified by the songs and music that punctuate the drama. With its interwoven plot lines – Prospero's revenge, Miranda's love story and Caliban's rebellion – *The Tempest* is at root musical, its richness on stage arising from an endlessly shifting kaleidoscope of symmetries, repetitions and contrasts. The magic depends on the effect of resonance and strangeness. The characters must be seen to stray into a world of hidden patterns, mysterious events and surprising encounters.

The play is comparatively simple to stage, though much depends on how ambitiously the three spectacular scenes are approached, and it is always necessary to have adequate musical resources. The sophisticated musical requirements were well suited to the Blackfriars theatre for which *The Tempest* was originally written, and Shakespeare must have been confident that he had a boy actor whose vocal talents could cope with the demands of Ariel's part. Staging at the Blackfriars (which was an intimate roofed playhouse serving wealthy but fairly small audiences) was probably relatively restrained, the impression of splendour being conveyed by the combination of poetry, song, dance and costume rather than elaborate scenic effects. Still, there would have been some scenic contribution, if not quite illusionistic scenery in the modern manner. Prospero's cell and Caliban's rock are several times mentioned, and while these spots could have been symbolized by the stage doors, it is possible that they were represented by free-standing scenic structures. There had to be a discovery space, concealed by a curtain, for Ferdinand and Miranda to be found in playing chess in Act V, and a 'line' is needed for the clothes set out to tempt Caliban's friends at IV.1.193. Flying effects are called for in Act IV and (perhaps) Act III, scene 2, and a gallery or upper area was necessary from which Prospero could oversee the harpy scene (see III.3.17). Props are significant: the logs that Caliban carries in Act I, scene 2 recur on Ferdinand's shoulders in Act III, scene 1, while Prospero's magic power is signalled by his staff, his powerlessness by his adoption of a rapier at V.1.84. Many of the play's most characteristic effects are contrasts of costume: between Prospero's magic gown, the goddesses' gorgeous robes, the 'trumpery' left out for the fools (IV.1.186), the court clothes worn by the aristo-

crats and eventually reassumed by Prospero, Caliban's
gaberdine, the fantastic costumes of Ariel and the spirits
(however they looked). Such symbolic contrasts would
have been readily appreciated by Shakespeare's audiences,
for in the early seventeenth century fabrics were reas-
suringly expensive.

Inevitably, *The Tempest* has always been prone to scenic
'improvement', directors often supplementing or
enlarging what Shakespeare calls for. In the eighteenth
and nineteenth centuries it became a machine-play par
excellence, with spectacular shipwrecks, thunder and
lightning, realistic seascapes and forbidding mountainous
shores, extra ballets and flying effects. The frontispiece
to Nicholas Rowe's 1709 edition shows the ship labouring
in waves with dragons and devils in the clouds above,
while in William Macready's 1838 production, the ship
was assaulted by demons that descended from the
heavens. Charles Kean's 1857 revival had a crew of thirty
running around the deck in thunderous noise and fury.
Hans Christian Andersen saw this production and was
impressed by the 'great waves ... rolling toward the
footlights' until 'the masts fell, and then the ship
was swallowed up by the sea' (quoted in Christine
Dymkowski, ed., *The Tempest* (2000), p. 74). For audiences in these years, the staging of the storm was always
a highlight, and the custom eventually arose of relying
on spectacle alone in the storm scene and cutting
Shakespeare's words altogether.

For reasons of both aesthetics and expense, the modern
trend has been towards barer stages and minimalist design,
conveying the storm through sound, movement or
symbolism. A typical example was Peter Brook's 1957
Stratford-upon-Avon production, which suggested the
waves' effect of vertigo with a huge lantern swinging

hypnotically from side to side, sailors climbing in the rigging, and unnerving sonic alterations between roaring noise and perfect silence. In the acclaimed Italian production by Giorgio Strehler (Milan, 1978), giant waves were created by billowing blue cloth into which the courtiers sank and out of which the flat raised square of the island eventually emerged. In Ron Daniels' 1982 Royal Shakespeare Company revival, the skeleton of the wrecked ship was left onstage after the storm and became the location for the rest of the action. An important choice in any production is whether the storm is allowed to seem the work of nature, or whether Ariel or Prospero is brought onstage, an addition that admits at the outset that the waves have really been artificially created.

Other aspects of the play have also been elaborated. Shakespeare's text was early on dislodged from the stage by an adaptation by William Davenant and John Dryden, *The Enchanted Island* (1667), which turned it in an operatic direction. More eventful action was added and new characters introduced – notably, Miranda and Caliban each acquired a sister. From this adaptation, further versions were made, which permitted symmetrical flying (by giving Ariel a partner, Milcha) and added dozens of songs. Shakespeare's text gradually returned in the nineteenth century, but the play has continued to attract the attention of composers, from Thomas Arne to Jean Sibelius, Michael Tippett and Thomas Adès (whose fully operatic version premiered in 2004). Musically, the staging of Act IV is always a test for modern directors, who need to find an idiom which substitutes for the conventions of Jacobean court masque without falling into styles that are either kitsch or underwhelming. The most elaborate recent treatment was the mini-opera incorporated into Daniels' 1982 production, in which the entire masque was set to music and culminated with Ferdinand and Miranda joining in the dancing. Other enthusiastically celebratory versions include the Brazilian carnival devised for the New York Shakespeare Festival in 1995, the aerial ballet by trapeze dancers seen at the RSC in 2002 and the campy crew of dancing sailors who round off Derek Jarman's film version (1980).

However, some otherwise successful productions have come badly unstuck when handling the masque, and frequently directors prefer to treat it ironically, allowing it to be distanced by elements of parody and pastiche. For example, Sam Mendes' 1993 RSC version staged it in a replica Victorian theatre like a pop-up book, with the performers adopting deliberately puppet-like movements, while in Jonathan Miller's 1988 Old Vic production a political point was made by the contrast between the African performers in beads, skirts and masks and the incongruously baroque music which they sang. Directors also often incorporate explanations for the masque's unexpected collapse. In Strehler's production drumbeats were heard offstage, and in Keith Hack's 1974 RSC revival there were shouts of 'Freedom' and 'Caliban'. Caliban himself invaded the masque and carried off Juno during Michael Bogdanov's production (English Shakespeare Company, 1992). More sinisterly, in Sam Mendes' revival, Caliban was revealed to be dancing amongst the reapers. It is, though, just as effective to leave the reason for the interruption as a puzzle, or to locate it in Prospero's inexplicable anxieties. In Michael Boyd's production (RSC 2002), Prospero seemed to have been upset by the erotic suggestiveness of the dancing itself.

By contrast, directors have found the vanishing banquet easier to deal with, for stage tricks such as reversible tables can readily be devised to whisk the food away, and Ariel's entry as a harpy allows a visual effect which is simple yet shocking. A flying Ariel will always impress, like Scott Handy in Adrian Noble's 1998 RSC production, whose huge red wings made him seem like some 'dangerous angel breathing fire and brimstone' (Nicholas de Jongh, *Evening Standard*, 26 February 1998). But simpler devices can be equally startling: for the RSC in 1993, Simon Russell Beale erupted from below the table in a blood-stained costume, looking to the critics like 'a waiter who had eaten one of the diners' (Peter Holland, *English Shakespeares* (1997), p. 172). The only recurrent problem seems to be how to make the '*strange Shapes*' (III.3.17) appear strange without descending into cliché or bathos.

For the play's overall interpretation, the three crucial roles are Prospero, Ariel and Caliban. Given the size of Prospero's part, performances depend to an unusual degree on a single actor, but the three characters are so inextricably linked that a shift in any one of them tends to necessitate a corresponding adjustment in the other two. Much of the play's potential on the stage can be described in terms of changes to the balance between these parts.

For generations the belief prevailed that Prospero was a relatively straightforward figure, a mysterious genius, dignified prophet or benign schoolmaster whose character presented little moral ambiguity. Indeed, for a long time Prospero's lack of complexity was the play's Achilles' heel. He provoked respect but no real interest, as there seemed little inner journey for him to accomplish. He could easily appear pompous and verbose, or dreamy and other-worldly – as one reviewer once put it, 'the usual combination of Father Christmas, a colonial bishop, and president of the Magicians' Union' (cited in

Dymkowski, p. 19). This began to change in the late nineteenth century, largely in response to a new interest in Caliban's qualities as more than a mere monster. Caliban was treated as the real star part in the productions by Frank Benson (Stratford, 1891) and Herbert Beerbohm Tree (His Majesty's Theatre, 1904), and as a consequence of this shift Prospero's flaws started to emerge more clearly. It is still possible today for Prospero to appear serene and sweet, wise and caring, acting in the best interests of daughter and state, genuinely loved by his family and admired by his friends. But the dialectic with his less admirable qualities is now always part of the equation. His irascibility, impatience, arbitrariness, aloofness and quickness to suspicion have to be acknowledged, if not accommodated. For the actor, this change has revivified the role. It makes Prospero's part a struggle for mastery over himself and a search for conviction about the worth of the journey that he is making.

The key modern performances were those of Sir John Gielgud, who played Prospero four times on the stage and once in film (in Peter Greenaway's *Prospero's Books*), in the process moving him into a new dimension. Gielgud's Prosperos were not comfortable but bitter. A vigorous, forceful and intellectually alert individual, he always dominated the play, but was not easily likeable. He was stately and melancholy, but his outward calm conflicted with hints of cruelty and his brooding on the past. He often seemed close to being overwhelmed by resentment and too keen on vengeance, and he needed to rein in his potential selfishness, so that the final resolution always appeared hard-won. A similar conception was played by Ian Richardson (RSC, 1970), who seemed weary, cold and withdrawn, and Derek Jacobi (RSC, 1982), who fluctuated unpredictably between aggression and lyricism, revengefulness and contrition. More humane Prosperos, who are happier to forgive, have included Michael Hordern's quiet, simply dressed father figure (RSC, 1978), and Michael Redgrave (Stratford-upon-Avon, 1951), for whom the magic was an exhausting effort. The two sides of the role were perhaps most fully yoked in John Wood's portrayal (RSC, 1988). Wood made Prospero kindly, tender, warm and gentle, loving with Miranda, desperate for affection even from Antonio, yet prone to sudden rages, inept in his relations with those around him, and rather lonely and childlike. Still intensely pained by the memory of the trauma that had swept him from Milan, he was as much the victim as the victor. Such widely varying interpretations amply suggest the possibilities latent in the role. The play takes its emotional energy from Prospero's inner demons, the unresolved attitudes of forgiveness, pain and reproach between which he is perpetually torn.

With Caliban, the main performance question concerns how he is to be represented: whether he is a recognizably human character whose monstrosity resides in the eyes of those who encounter him, or whether he has animal or non-human features that make him seem incorrigibly alien. Directors have often seized on one aspect of the text and allowed that to define him. Many Calibans, picking up from Trinculo's 'A man or a fish?' (II.2.25), have been fishy or reptilian, with (variously) scaly skin, fins, webbed hands and feet and darting tongue. There have also been many apes or Darwinian missing links. In the 1890s, Frank Benson made a big impact playing Caliban as 'half-monkey, half-coconut', arriving with a real fish in his mouth and performing vigorous zoological acrobatics. Gielgud's second Prospero (Old Vic, 1940) had Jack Hawkins as a monkey Caliban with a tail, while Alec Clunes played him at Stratford in 1957 as a sad pet-like gorilla. The tendency of this approach is to confirm Caliban's status as a comic or subhuman figure. He has also been a semi-demonic wild man, like the snarling, taloned creature seen in William Burton's 1854 New York production, or William Poel's long-haired grotesque (London, 1897), or Herbert Beerbohm Tree's semi-werewolf (1904), with fangs for teeth, unkempt hair, shaggy torso, uncut nails and seaweed skirt. Tree's Caliban grovelled and crawled around the stage, though he was acutely sensitive to music, and the play ended with a tableau intended to show his pathos, as he crept sadly from his rock to watch Prospero's ship sailing away. This was a Caliban whose master had shown him a better life and without whom he had lost his reason for living.

Twentieth-century Calibans have increasingly emphasized the human being in the monster, or seen him as a misrecognized human, victimized by his fellows. The first Caliban to be blacked up appeared at the Old Vic in 1934, and the first black actor to play Caliban was Canada Lee in New York, 1945. The play received its most thorough-going colonial reading to date in Jonathan Miller's Mermaid Theatre production (1980), with both Caliban and Ariel played by black actors. Miller strongly suggested that Caliban's degradation was due to his slavery, whereas Ariel, the mulatto house servant, had learned the arts of power from his master and took control when the Europeans departed. However, one problem with racializing Caliban's otherness is that it runs the risk of implying that Caliban is dangerous because he is black. This was certainly the case with Roy Dotrice's blacked-up Caliban in 1963 (RSC), where reviewers blithely took his skin colour as just another marker of savagery, and responses were also mixed for the RSC's 1974 production, reviewers feeling that the play's stigmatizing of Caliban's 'monstrosity' was crudely offensive to the handsome black actor Jeffrey Kissoon. The most powerful performance in this tradition was probably David Suchet's in 1978. This Caliban succeeded because he combined different sorts of otherness and seemed a generalized image of oppression without specific racial identity. Dark-skinned, but with a lumpy bald skull, squashed nose and protruding forehead, and carrying a voodoo doll expressing his hatred of Prospero, he appeared as neither purely African, Indian nor aboriginal. His high point was his song of freedom, performed like a tribal dance celebrating his desire for liberty. Suchet has written interestingly about the experience of performing the part (see Further Reading).

Despite the prevalence of colonial readings in criticism, in the theatre Caliban has only occasionally been portrayed through racial stereotypes. The role can be made to work through allusions to any marginalized or demonized group, or simply as a generalized reflection on power and subordination. He has been a thalidomide child, a punk-rocker, a football hooligan and a Rastafarian. In an interesting if contrived effect, Dennis Quilley played Caliban at the National Theatre in 1974 as literally bisected: from one side his face and body showed the ugly monster that Prospero perceives, while from the other he was a noble savage. In Derek Jarman's film, Caliban is an eccentric blind manservant, and hardly any threat to Prospero; the effect of this is to make the real problem appear to lie not with him but with Prospero's obsession with magic. At the National Theatre in 1988, Tony Haygarth's Caliban was a nearly naked devil with short horns on his forehead, and his genitalia were padlocked into an ugly and painful metal chastity belt. For the RSC in 1993, David Troughton played Caliban as a disturbing albino wrestler, bald, white and crouching, who seemed both simple and dangerous, human in appearance yet with powerful animal instincts that could not safely be controlled. The sheer plenitude of options demonstrates the play's openness, the way that its images of obedience and rebellion can work in almost any possible context. And since the text leaves it unclear whether Caliban stays on the island or is taken by Prospero to Milan, his story can also be concluded in a variety of ways.

With Ariel there is also a wide spectrum of possibilities, for the text is even vaguer about his appearance than Caliban's. Most modern Ariels have been athletic young men, their identity as a spirit suggested by their near nakedness – as with Ben Kingsley (RSC, 1970) and Scott Handy (RSC, 1998), both of whom wore merely a loincloth and had white painted bodies – or their other-worldly clothing, such as the bodysuit covered with veins and arteries worn by Mark Rylance (RSC, 1982). Sometimes Ariel is only the leader of a group of spirits – Rylance had a gang of followers, as did Ian Holm in 1963 (RSC) – though such devices run the risk of interrupting the focus on his directly personal relationship with Prospero. Most Ariels move swiftly in service of Prospero, but sometimes their other-worldliness is conveyed by a deliberate slowness of movement, as was the case with Ian Holm, Ian Charleson (RSC, 1978), Olwen Fouéré (English Shakespeare Company, 1992) and Simon Russell Beale (RSC, 1993). Such a choice suggests Ariel's self-possession, but can also make him appear sinister or reluctant. The pay-off comes in the final moments, when Ariel escapes eagerly into the life that he has been waiting for.

Yet Ariel does not have to be a man, for in the stage

tradition reaching back to the eighteenth century the part has more commonly been played by women. This custom was dislodged only in the early twentieth century and has shown signs of returning in recent productions. The female Ariels come out of a time when the play was enjoyed as much for music and spectacle as for drama. Many of these Ariels were fairy figures, with gauzy costumes, gossamer gowns and delicate wings. Their performances were balletic, often literally aerial, and their attitude was generally submissive. One effect of casting a woman is to underline the parallelism with Miranda, drawing attention to the combination of love and subordination that both experience (Rachel Sanderson played Ariel as a moody teenager for Shared Experience in 1996). Male Ariels, on the other hand, tend to invite comparisons with Caliban, and bring issues of obedience and rebellion under closer scrutiny. And another variable for Ariel is his/her age. In Shakespeare's Blackfriars, Ariel would have been played by an adolescent boy (who, in the conventions of the time, took female parts in the plays; hence Miranda too was 'really' a boy). If played by a child, Ariel becomes another member of Prospero's family, his dependence and eagerness to please being part of the dynamic of growing up on the island, and it drains his role of tension, leading towards mere fantasy by presenting him as an elf or 'tricksy spirit' (V.1.226). No Ariel – as far as I am aware – has ever been of very advanced years, but it remains true that the older Ariels get the more their moodiness and desire for independence registers. The ultimate example of this tendency was Simon Russell Beale's baleful, detached Ariel, who clearly did not reciprocate the love that Prospero felt for him. At thirty-two, Beale was one of the oldest Ariels of recent times.

The delicate, changeful relationship between Prospero and Ariel is one means by which the play fills out the magician's secretive emotional life. Without Ariel, we would see even less of the private man. The older tradition was to emphasize Prospero's commanding mastery over the spirit. Gielgud, for example, never looked directly at Ariel, and narrated the story of his imprisonment with sadistic relish (though he is more kindly in the film *Prospero's Books*, where there are four Ariels, all of different ages). As modern portrayals have registered more fully Ariel's desire to be free, so they have complicated the emotional bond with Prospero, and the extent of the master's dependence on the servant, or the degree to which Prospero takes him for granted. Several Ariels have clearly felt unloved, giving emphasis to the line 'Do you love me, master? No?' (IV.1.48) or implying at the end that they feel Prospero is abandoning them. Others have kept themselves hidden – in the 1998 RSC version, David Calder's Prospero never saw Ariel, and knew of his presence only through an electric shock that he received when they occasionally touched – while some Ariels have departed from the stage before Prospero's dismissal, leaving the master vainly striving to affirm a relationship that has already been severed. As with Caliban's promise to 'seek for grace' (V.1.296) or Antonio's silent response to Prospero's forgiveness (130–34), the signals that pass between Ariel and Prospero in the final moments can suggest that the story is far from resolved. The play offers no one ending, but a range of closures, from happy reunion to regretful departure to recovery tinged with enduring loss.

Further Reading

The Tempest has been fortunate with its editors and benefits from first-rate editions. Of the older texts, Frank Kermode's Arden second series edition (1954) stands up best, being valuable for the detail of its notes and breadth of its introduction. Kermode attends to the play's intellectual contexts, offering a learned account of magic, art and nature, even if his view of Prospero now seems rather idealizing. The introduction to Anne Barton's New Penguin Shakespeare edition (1968), in the predecessor series to the present volume, eloquently explores the play's open-endedness and imaginative resonance, and has one of the best analyses of its language.

Radical new directions were signalled by Stephen Orgel's Oxford edition (1987), the introduction to which Orgel trailed in a seminal essay, 'Prospero's wife', published in Margaret W. Ferguson, Maureen Quilligan and Nancy J. Vickers, eds., *Rewriting the Renaissance* (1986). This was the first edition to register the changes in critical theory that were occurring in the 1980s. Orgel shifted the emphasis from Prospero's ethical intentions to his political purpose, exploring his dynastic plans and questioning his power and its difference from Sycorax's magic. Orgel's edition acknowledges emerging post-colonial perspectives on Caliban, but particularly foregrounds the sexual politics and the play's 'absent' characters, especially Prospero's dead wife and her significance for his identity as duke and father. This valuable edition has been the starting point for much subsequent critical work.

Succeeding editions have not stood still but demonstrate the play's continuing richness and appeal. The Arden third series text, edited by A. T. Vaughan and V. M. Vaughan (1999), emphasizes the play's afterlife in adaptations and spin-offs. David Lindley's New Cambridge edition (2002) has excellent notes and a searching introduction that questions many of the clichés that have crept into discussion. He roots interpretation in examples from performance and has much the best account of the play's music, a topic he also handles in an essay, 'Music, masque and meaning in *The Tempest*', in *The Court Masque*, ed. Lindley (1984), pp. 47–59. Also useful is the Norton Critical Edition, eds. Peter Hulme and William H. Sherman (2004). This is lightly annotated but accompanies the text with a selection of critical essays and extracts from poetic and theatrical rewritings based on the play.

The play's source materials, including William Strachey's *A True Reportory of the Wrack*, are reprinted in Geoffrey Bullough's *Narrative and Dramatic Sources of Shakespeare*, vol. VIII (1975). The play's backgrounds in Ovid and Virgil are usefully discussed in Jonathan Bate's *Shakespeare and Ovid* (1993) and Heather James's *Shakespeare's Troy* (1997). Helen Cooper has an excellent account of its relation to romance literature in *The English Romance in Time* (2004); her analysis focuses on its structural symmetries and on the romance quest as an ethical allegory. The play's language is analysed in detail in Russ McDonald's essay 'Reading *The Tempest*', *Shakespeare*

Survey 43 (1991), pp. 15–28, and in Simon Palfrey's *Late Shakespeare: A New World of Words* (1997). Prospero's magic is discussed by Barbara A. Mowat in two important essays, 'Prospero, Agrippa and Hocus Pocus', *English Literary Renaissance* 11 (1981), pp. 281–303, and 'Prospero's Book', *Shakespeare Quarterly* 52 (2001), pp. 1–33, the latter looking at surviving early modern examples of 'grimoires' (practical instruction books for the control of spirits).

Of the older critical studies, Harry Berger Jr.'s essay 'Miraculous harp: a reading of Shakespeare's *The Tempest*', *Shakespeare Studies* 5 (1969), pp. 253–83, now looks much the most searching. He presents the old view of Prospero as essentially an artist, but his account is many-sided, refusing to take Prospero at his own valuation, asking awkward questions about his intentions and his effect on those around him. In many ways, though in a different register, Berger anticipates the more overtly politicized criticism to come twenty years later.

The first sign of a critical shift came in psychoanalytical studies published in the 1980s. The best examples are in the collection *Representing Shakespeare* (1980), eds. Murray M. Schwartz and Coppélia Kahn. David Sundelson's essay 'So rare a wonder'd father: Prospero's *Tempest*' presents Prospero as the play's controlling ego, and explores the psychic dynamics of his home life, stressing issues of parenting, pleasure and authority. Coppélia Kahn's 'The providential tempest and the Shakespearean family' reads the play as Prospero's fantasy of omnipotence, and sees him as working through Oedipal tensions and conflicted feelings. A similar tack is followed in Ruth Nevo's *Shakespeare's Other Language* (1987), which sees the play as wish-fulfilment in which Prospero discharges anxieties about sibling rivalry and

his daughter's growing up, and in Janet Adelman's
Suffocating Mothers (1992), which views the plot as
Prospero's response to the psychic threat of the maternal.
As a group, these studies put paid to the idea of Prospero
as the benevolent, selfless father, presenting instead a hero
riven by tension and conflict. Their emphasis on the
suppression of psychological anxieties reinforced readings of Prospero as a politically repressive figure that
were starting to emerge elsewhere.

At the same time as this work, interest was developing
in the play's relationship to early modern discovery and
colonial activity, and the impact that it subsequently had
on the imagining of empire. Scholarly discussion of this
topic goes back to the first Arden edition, ed. Morton
Luce (1902), and Sidney Lee's *Life of Shakespeare* (rev.
1923), but it opened out in the 1970s and 80s under the
influence of the emergent post-colonial criticism. Two
early essays were Charles Frey's '*The Tempest* and the
New World', *Shakespeare Quarterly* 30 (1979), pp. 29–41,
which looked at the play's roots in travel literature, and
Trevor R. Griffiths' '"This island's mine": Caliban and
colonialism', *The Yearbook of English Studies* 13 (1983),
pp. 159–80, which traced colonial perspectives back to
the nineteenth-century stage. But the political high
ground was seized by three nearly simultaneous publi-
cations: Paul Brown's '"This thing of darkness I acknowledge mine": *The Tempest* and the discourse of
colonialism', in Jonathan Dollimore and Alan Sinfield,
eds., *Political Shakespeare* (1985), pp. 48–71; Francis
Barker and Peter Hulme's 'Nymphs and reapers heavily
vanish: the discursive con-texts of *The Tempest*', in John
Drakakis, ed., *Alternative Shakespeares* (1985), pp.
191–205; and Peter Hulme's *Colonial Encounters* (1986).
All of these essays presented *The Tempest* as embedded

in England's overseas expansion and saw the story as allegorizing colonial relations. Another influence was Stephen Greenblatt's argument in 'Invisible Bullets' (in the Dollimore/Sinfield collection), for Brown, Barker and Hulme all see Prospero's treatment of Caliban as of a piece with the relationships of surveillance, domination and mastery which (Greenblatt argued) characterized early modern political discourse. *The Tempest* was thus symptomatic of the chains of imperialism that Shakespeare's theatre could not help but affirm. Greenblatt himself discusses Prospero as a colonist of the mind in *Shakespearean Negotiations* (1988), and in *Learning to Curse* (1990) he suggests that Caliban is imprisoned in a discourse 'owned' by his colonizer.

There followed a rich flood of post-colonial criticism, of which only the highlights can be listed: Ania Loomba's *Gender, Race, Renaissance Drama* (1989); Jeffrey Knapp's *An Empire Nowhere* (1992); John Gillies' *Shakespeare and the Geography of Difference* (1994); Kim F. Hall's *Things of Darkness* (1995); and Joan Pong Linton's *The Romance of the New World* (1998). Caliban has been the focus of several books. V. M. Vaughan and A. T. Vaughan's *Shakespeare's Caliban: A Cultural History* (1991) surveys in great detail the sources for him and his various materializations on the stage and in literary spin-offs to the present day. Harold Bloom's *Caliban* (1992) is an anthology of criticism about him. In *Constellation Caliban* (1997) Nadia Lie and Theo D'haen focus on twentieth-century rewritings of him. In *Constructing Monsters in Shakespearean Drama and Early Modern Culture* (2003), Mark Thornton Burnett situates Caliban in relation to the cult of monstrosity and strange sights.

This criticism eventually met a backlash from scholars who felt that some of the earlier essays were inattentive to the historical specifics of colonial enterprise, projecting a politics back onto the play that really derived from a later imperialism, and forgetting that Prospero never intended to go to the island. The most substantial critique along these lines is Meredith Anne Skura's 'Discourse and the individual: the case of colonialism in *The Tempest*', *Shakespeare Quarterly* 40 (1989), pp. 191–209, which takes some post-colonial readings to task for anachronism. A critique from within the post-colonial camp comes from Jerry Brotton, '"This Tunis, sir, was Carthage": contesting colonialism in *The Tempest*', in *Post-Colonial Shakespeares*, eds. Ania Loomba and Martin Orkin (1998), pp. 23–42. Brotton argues that many discussions forget the importance of the southern Mediterranean frontier, that the island belongs to a trading economy with North Africa and the Islamic Middle East which was more significant than trade across the Atlantic. The North African background is also filled in by Barbara Fuchs in 'Conquering islands: contextualizing *The Tempest*', *Shakespeare Quarterly* 48 (1997), pp. 45–62, and by Richard Wilson in *Secret Shakespeare* (2004). Another challenging essay of this kind is in David Scott Kastan's *Shakespeare After Theory* (1999), which argues that the play is linked more closely to the affairs of contemporary Italian and middle European princely states than to America. Kastan finds analogies for Prospero's exile and Miranda's marriage in the recent history of kingly families much closer to home.

Another powerful challenge comes from those critics who feel that the post-colonial model can be excessively imperial and dystopian, especially if it represents Shakespeare colluding with princely power, as if no other politics could be imagined. In '"What cares these roarers for the name of king?": language and utopia in *The*

Tempest', in *The Politics of Tragicomedy*, eds. Gordon McMullan and Jonathan Hope (1992), pp. 21–54, David Norbrook finds a republican subtext in detailed analysis of the characters' speech-acts. He explores the play's intellectual background, relating it to Montaigne and to traditions of utopian and libertarian writing. In his hands, the subtle differentiations between the characters' various languages emerge very strongly. Another strenuous critique comes from Richard Strier in '"I am power": normal and magical politics in *The Tempest*', in Derek Hirst and Richard Strier, eds., *Writing and Political Engagement in Seventeenth-Century England* (1999), pp. 10–30. Strier looks at contemporary ideas of master–servant relationships, and turns post-colonial discourse inside out. His Prospero is a failed colonist, someone with 'grave lack of sociability combined with a pathological urge to dominate'.

Work on sex and gender has been no less fertile. Feminist critics have pursued parallel insights, since their interest in Prospero's mastery of Miranda reinforces the post-colonial critique of Caliban. Thus Lorie Jerrell Leininger's 'The Miranda trap: sexism and racism in Shakespeare's *Tempest*', in Carolyn Lenz et al., *The Woman's Part* (1980), pp. 285–94, presents Miranda as a helpless victim of Prospero's power. Ann Thompson's '"Miranda, where's your sister?": Reading Shakespeare's *The Tempest*', in *Feminist Criticism: Theory and Practice*, ed. Susan Sellers (1991), pp. 45–55, is also uncomfortable with the play, seeing Miranda as symbolically central yet essentially passive and dependent. Such terms make a 'feminist' *Tempest* problematic, if not impossible. A more besetting difficulty is outlined by Jyotsna G. Singh in 'Caliban versus Miranda: race and gender conflicts in postcolonial rewritings of *The Tempest*', in *Feminist*

Readings of Early Modern Culture: Emerging Subjects, eds. Valerie Traub, M. Lindsay Kaplan and Dympna Callaghan (1996), pp. 191–209. Singh notes that feminist and post-colonial readings of the play are often at odds, since as the white man's property Miranda is the object of Caliban's aspirations, his political ambitions running against her (the potential rape victim) rather than in concert. Singh finds this tension in the play and in many of its twentieth-century rewritings. Of course, such disputes between feminist and post-colonial criticism are not confined to *The Tempest*.

The play's other women have received attention. In *The Witch in History* (1996), Diane Purkiss analyses Sycorax as a projection of early modern anxieties about powerful women. Marina Warner also treats Sycorax in '"The foul witch" and her "freckled whelp": Circean mutations in the New World', in the collection *'The Tempest' and its Travels*, eds. Peter Hulme and William H. Sherman (2000), pp. 97–113. Claribel and the Prince of Tunis are discussed by Marjorie Raley in 'Claribel's husband', in *Race, Ethnicity and Power in the Renaissance*, ed. Joyce Green MacDonald (1997), pp. 95–119. Linda Bamber supplies Claribel's letters home in 'Claribel at Palace dot Tunis', in Marianne Novy, ed., *Transforming Shakespeare: Contemporary Women's Re-Visions in Literature and Performance* (1999), pp. 237–57, telling us what really happened after Prospero sailed back to Milan.

Currently a growth area is work on the play's afterlife, its many adaptations and rewritings. Rob Nixon's 'Caribbean and African appropriations of *The Tempest*', *Critical Inquiry* 13 (1987), pp. 557–78, Thomas Cartelli's *Repositioning Shakespeare* (1999) and Jonathan Goldberg's *Tempest in the Caribbean* (2004) discuss works by African,

Caribbean and South American writers. Rewritings by women, and Derek Jarman's film version, are considered by Kate Chedgzoy in *Shakespeare's Queer Children* (1995). Marina Warner's novel *Indigo* is analysed by Caroline Cakebread in Novy, ed., *Transforming Shakespeare*, pp. 217–36. In *'The Tempest' and its Travels*, Hulme and Sherman collect essays on stage productions, literary rewritings and visual art based on the play. Chantal Zabus's *Tempests after Shakespeare* (2002) ranges across writing and films from Latin America, the Caribbean, Europe, Africa, Australia and beyond. Peter Greenaway's film version is discussed by Martin Butler in 'Prospero in Cyberspace', in *Re-constructing the Book* (2001), eds. Maureen Bell et al., pp. 184–96.

The play's stage history is treated in two excellent books: Christine Dymkowski's *The Tempest* in the Shakespeare in Production series (2000), an edition with annotation from prompt books, reviews and eyewitness accounts, which supplies much detail about the performance of scenes, characters and even single lines; and David Lindley's *The Tempest* in the Shakespeare at Stratford series (2003), which confines itself to Royal Shakespeare Company revivals but offers rich analyses of widely contrasting interpretations and has many insights about staging issues that affect all productions. David Suchet has written eloquently about Caliban from the performer's perspective in *Players of Shakespeare: I*, ed. Philip Brockbank (1989). David L. Hirst's *The Tempest: Text and Performance* (1984) and Roger Warren's *Staging Shakespeare's Late Plays* (1990) give general theatre-based overviews, Warren's drawing on his experience of working on the play with Peter Hall in 1988. Arthur Horowitz's *Prospero's 'True Preservers'* (2004) describes landmark productions by Peter Brook, Yukio Ninagawa and Giorgio Strehler. The original staging of 1611 is discussed by Andrew Gurr in '*The Tempest*'s tempest at Blackfriars', *Shakespeare Survey 41* (1989), pp. 91–102.

Finally, there are some good anthologies of essays, most recently A. T. Vaughan and V. M. Vaughan, eds., *Critical Essays on Shakespeare's 'The Tempest'* (1998), and R. S. White, ed., *The Tempest* in the New Casebooks series (1999).

THE TEMPEST

The Characters in the Play

ALONSO, King of Naples
SEBASTIAN, his brother
PROSPERO, the right Duke of Milan
ANTONIO, his brother, the usurping Duke of Milan
FERDINAND, son to the King of Naples
GONZALO, an honest old councillor
ADRIAN and FRANCISCO, lords
CALIBAN, a savage and deformed slave
TRINCULO, a jester
STEPHANO, a drunken butler
MASTER of a ship
BOATSWAIN
MARINERS
MIRANDA, daughter to Prospero
ARIEL, an airy spirit
IRIS
CERES
JUNO } spirits in the masque
NYMPHS
REAPERS
Other spirits, courtiers

The scene, an uninhabited island

A tempestuous noise of thunder and lightning heard
Enter a Shipmaster and a Boatswain

MASTER Boatswain!

BOATSWAIN Here, Master. What cheer?

MASTER Good, speak to th'mariners. Fall to't yarely, or
we run ourselves aground. Bestir, bestir!   *Exit*
Enter Mariners

BOATSWAIN Hey, my hearts! Cheerly, cheerly my hearts!
Yare, yare! Take in the topsail! Tend to th'Master's
whistle. (*To the storm*) Blow till thou burst thy wind, if
room enough!
Enter Alonso, Sebastian, Antonio, Ferdinand,
Gonzalo, and others

ALONSO Good Boatswain, have care. Where's the Master?
Play the men.   10

BOATSWAIN I pray now, keep below.

ANTONIO Where is the Master, Boatswain?

BOATSWAIN Do you not hear him? You mar our labour.
Keep your cabins! You do assist the storm.

GONZALO Nay, good, be patient.

BOATSWAIN When the sea is. Hence! What cares these
roarers for the name of king? To cabin! Silence! Trouble
us not.

GONZALO Good, yet remember whom thou hast aboard.

All for themselves.
Doesn't care about the king being on board.

20 BOATSWAIN None that I more love than myself. You are
a councillor; if you can command these elements to
silence and work the peace of the present, we will not
hand a rope more, use your authority. If you cannot,
give thanks you have lived so long, and make yourself
ready in your cabin for the mischance of the hour, if
it so hap. – (*To the sailors*) Cheerly, good hearts! – Out
of our way, I say.   *Exit*

GONZALO I have great comfort from this fellow. Methinks
he hath no drowning mark upon him, his complexion

30 is perfect gallows. Stand fast, good Fate, to his hanging;
make the rope of his destiny our cable, for our own
doth little advantage. If he be not born to be hanged,
our case is miserable.   *Exeunt courtiers*

Enter Boatswain

BOATSWAIN Down with the topmast! Yare! Lower, lower!
Bring her to try with main-course.

A cry within

A plague upon this howling! They are louder than the
weather, or our office.

Enter Sebastian, Antonio, and Gonzalo

Yet again? What do you here? Shall we give o'er and
drown? Have you a mind to sink?

40 SEBASTIAN A pox o'your throat, you bawling, blasphemous, incharitable dog! — Having a go right back.

BOATSWAIN Work you, then!

ANTONIO Hang cur, hang, you whoreson insolent noise-
maker! We are less afraid to be drowned than thou art.

GONZALO I'll warrant him for drowning, though the ship
were no stronger than a nutshell, and as leaky as an
unstanched wench.

BOATSWAIN Lay her a-hold, a-hold! Set her two courses
off to sea again, lay her off!

Enter Mariners, wet

[Marginalia, left: Change of opinion. Agrees with Boats.]

[Marginalia, left: Suggesting that he is a coward. Totally willing to die for the king.]

MARINERS All lost! To prayers, to prayers, all lost!   50
BOATSWAIN What, must our mouths be <u>cold</u>?

GONZALO
The King and Prince at prayers! Let's assist them,
For our case is as theirs.

SEBASTIAN   I'm out of patience.

ANTONIO
We are merely cheated of our lives by drunkards.
This wide-chopped rascal, would thou mightst lie
    drowning
The washing of ten tides.

GONZALO   He'll be hanged yet,
Though every drop of water swear against it,
And gape at wid'st to glut him.

    A confused noise within

           Mercy on us!

VOICES OFFSTAGE
We split, we split! Farewell, my wife and children!
Farewell, brother! We split, we split, we split!   60

ANTONIO
Let's all sink wi'th'King.

SEBASTIAN   Let's take leave of him.

    Exeunt Antonio and Sebastian

GONZALO Now would I give a thousand furlongs of sea
for an acre of barren ground – long heath, brown furze,
anything! The wills above be done, but I would fain
die a dry death.   *Exit*

    Enter Prospero and Miranda   I.2

MIRANDA
If by your art, my dearest father, you have
Put the <u>wild waters</u> in this roar, allay them.
The sky it seems would pour down stinking pitch,

[handwritten top margin: Prospero: must have been a good guy to have a daughter like Miranda.]

But that the sea, mounting to th'welkin's cheek,
Dashes the fire out. O, I have suffered
With those that I saw suffer: a brave vessel,
Who had, no doubt, some noble creature in her,
Dashed all to pieces. O, the cry did knock
Against my very heart! Poor souls, they perished.

[handwritten left margin: Sheol save the ship. Compassion]

        Had I been any god of power, I would
Have sunk the sea within the earth or ere
It should the good ship so have swallowed, and
The fraughting souls within her.

PROSPERO   Be collected;

[handwritten left margin: he organised the attack]

No more amazement. Tell your piteous heart
There's no harm done. — *Revenge?*

MIRANDA   O, woe the day!

[handwritten left margin: Saying she doesn't really know who she is]

PROSPERO   No harm.
I have done nothing but in care of thee –
Of thee, my dear one, thee my daughter – who
Art ignorant of what thou art, naught knowing
Of whence I am, nor that I am more better
Than Prospero, master of a full poor cell,
And thy no greater father.

MIRANDA   . More to know
Did never meddle with my thoughts.

PROSPERO   'Tis time

[handwritten left margin: He has been hiding something bad from her]

I should inform thee further. Lend thy hand,
And pluck my magic garment from me.
    Miranda helps Prospero remove his gown
                        So,
Lie there, my art. – Wipe thou thine eyes; have comfort.
The direful spectacle of the wreck, which touched
The very virtue of compassion in thee,
I have with such provision in mine art
So safely ordered that there is no soul –
No, not so much perdition as an hair

Betid to any creature in the vessel
Which thou heard'st cry, which thou saw'st sink. Sit
    down,
For thou must now know further.

MIRANDA   You have often
Begun to tell me what I am, but stopped,
And left me to a bootless inquisition,
Concluding, 'Stay; not yet.'

PROSPERO   The hour's now come;
The very minute bids thee ope thine ear.
Obey, and be attentive. Canst thou remember
A time before we came unto this cell?
I do not think thou canst, for then thou wast not   40
Out three years old.

MIRANDA   Certainly, sir, I can.

PROSPERO
By what? By any other house or person?
Of anything the image, tell me, that
Hath kept with thy remembrance.

MIRANDA   'Tis far off,
And rather like a dream than an assurance
That my remembrance warrants. Had I not
Four or five women once, that tended me?

[handwritten note: Must be very special baby to have that many woman looking after her.]

PROSPERO
Thou hadst, and more, Miranda. But how is it
That this lives in thy mind? What seest thou else
In the dark backward and abysm of time?   50
If thou rememb'rest aught ere thou cam'st here,
How thou cam'st here thou mayst.

MIRANDA   But that I do not.

PROSPERO
Twelve year since, Miranda, twelve year since,
Thy father was the Duke of Milan and
A prince of power.

MIRANDA   Sir, are not you my father?

PROSPERO

Thy mother was a piece of virtue, and *inherited good things from her mother*

She said thou wast my daughter; and thy father

Was Duke of Milan; and his only heir

And princess, no worse issued.

MIRANDA   O the heavens!

60   What foul play had we, that we came from thence?

Or blessèd was't we did?

PROSPERO   Both, both, my girl.

By foul play, as thou sayst, were we heaved thence,

But blessedly holp hither.

MIRANDA   O, my heart bleeds

To think o'th'teen that I have turned you to,

Which is from my remembrance! Please you, further.

PROSPERO

My brother and thy uncle, called Antonio –

I pray thee mark me, that a brother should

Be so perfidious – he, whom next thyself

Of all the world I loved, and to him put   *was given some power which he abused.*

70   The manage of my state, as at that time

Through all the signories it was the first,

And Prospero the prime duke, being so reputed

In dignity, and for the liberal arts

Without a parallel; those being all my study,

The government I cast upon my brother,

And to my state grew stranger, being transported

And rapt in secret studies. Thy false uncle –

Dost thou attend me?

MIRANDA   Sir, most heedfully.

PROSPERO

Being once perfected how to grant suits,

80   How to deny them, who t'advance, and who

To trash for over-topping, new created

The creatures that were mine, I say, or changed 'em,
Or else new formed 'em; having both the key
Of officer and office, set all hearts i'th'state
To what tune pleased his ear, that now he was
The ivy which had hid my princely trunk,
And sucked my verdure out on't. Thou attend'st not!

MIRANDA O good sir, I do.

PROSPERO   I pray thee, mark me.
I thus neglecting worldly ends, all dedicated
To closeness and the bettering of my mind
With that which, but by being so retired,   90
O'er-prized all popular rate, in my false brother
Awaked an evil nature; and my trust,
Like a good parent, did beget of him
A falsehood, in its contrary as great
As my trust was – which had indeed no limit,
A confidence sans bound. He being thus lorded,
Not only with what my revenue yielded
But what my power might else exact, like one
Who, having into truth by telling of it,   100
Made such a sinner of his memory
To credit his own lie, he did believe
He was indeed the duke, out o'th'substitution
And executing th'outward face of royalty
With all prerogative. Hence his ambition growing –
Dost thou hear?

MIRANDA   Your tale, sir, would cure deafness.

PROSPERO
To have no screen between this part he played
And him he played it for, he needs will be
Absolute Milan. Me, poor man, my library
Was dukedom large enough. Of temporal royalties   110
He thinks me now incapable, confederates –
So dry he was for sway – wi'th'King of Naples

To give him annual tribute, do him homage,
Subject his coronet to his crown, and bend
The dukedom yet unbowed – alas, poor Milan! –
To most ignoble stooping.

MIRANDA   O the heavens!

PROSPERO
Mark his condition and th'event, then tell me
If this might be a brother.

MIRANDA   I should sin
To think but nobly of my grandmother. *> No good without bad?*
120   Good wombs have borne bad sons.

PROSPERO   Now the condition.
This King of Naples, being an enemy
To me inveterate, hearkens my brother's suit,
Which was, that he in lieu o'th'premises
Of homage and I know not how much tribute,
Should presently extirpate me and mine
Out of the dukedom, and confer fair Milan,
With all the honours, on my brother. Whereon,
A treacherous army levied, one midnight *Evil takes*
Fated to th'purpose, did Antonio open *place at night*
130   The gates of Milan, and i'th' dead of darkness
The ministers for th'purpose hurried thence
Me and thy crying self.

MIRANDA   Alack, for pity!
I not rememb'ring how I cried out then
Will cry it o'er again. It is a hint
That wrings mine eyes to't.

PROSPERO   Hear a little further,
And then I'll bring thee to the present business
Which now's upon's, without the which this story
Were most impertinent.

MIRANDA   Wherefore did they not
That hour destroy us?

PROSPERO   Well demanded, wench;
  My tale provokes that question. Dear, they durst not,   140
  So dear the love my people bore me; nor set
  A mark so bloody on the business, but
  With colours fairer painted their foul ends.
  In few, they hurried us aboard a barque,
  Bore us some leagues to sea, where they prepared
  A rotten carcass of a butt, not rigged,
  Nor tackle, sail, nor mast – the very rats
  Instinctively have quit it: there they hoist us
  To cry to th'sea that roared to us, to sigh
  To th'winds, whose pity sighing back again   150
  Did us but loving wrong.
MIRANDA   Alack, what trouble
  Was I then to you!
PROSPERO   O, a cherubin
  Thou wast that did preserve me. Thou didst smile,
  Infusèd with a fortitude from heaven,
  When I have decked the sea with drops full salt,
  Under my burden groaned, which raised in me
  An undergoing stomach to bear up
  Against what should ensue.
MIRANDA
  How came we ashore?
PROSPERO   By providence divine.
  Some food we had, and some fresh water, that   160
  A noble Neapolitan, Gonzalo,
  Out of his charity – who being then appointed
  Master of this design – did give us, with
  Rich garments, linens, stuffs, and necessaries
  Which since have steaded much. So of his gentleness,
  Knowing I loved my books, he furnished me
  From mine own library with volumes that
  I prize above my dukedom.

[Handwritten annotations in margin:]
Really not sea worthy.
She was the reason to put a fight up. to survive.
Even though Antonio thinks hes got the complete role their are still people who care.

MIRANDA   Would I might
But ever see that man.

PROSPERO   Now I arise.
170   Sit still, and hear the last of our sea-sorrow.
Here in this island we arrived, and here
Have I, thy schoolmaster, made thee more profit
Than other princes can, that have more time
For vainer hours, and tutors not so careful.

MIRANDA
Heavens thank you for't. And now I pray you, sir,
For still 'tis beating in my mind, your reason
For raising this sea-storm?

PROSPERO   Know thus far forth:
By accident most strange, bountiful Fortune,
Now my dear lady, hath mine enemies
180   Brought to this shore; and by my prescience
I find my zenith doth depend upon
A most auspicious star, whose influence
If now I court not, but omit, my fortunes
Will ever after droop. Here cease more questions.
Thou art inclined to sleep. 'Tis a good dullness,
And give it way; I know thou canst not choose.
     Miranda sleeps
Come away, servant, come! I am ready now.
Approach, my Ariel! Come!
     Enter Ariel

ARIEL
All hail, great master! Grave sir, hail! I come
190   To answer thy best pleasure, be't to fly,
To swim, to dive into the fire, to ride
On the curled clouds. To thy strong bidding, task
Ariel and all his quality.

PROSPERO   Hast thou, spirit,
Performed to point the tempest that I bade thee?

ARIEL

To every article.
I boarded the King's ship; now on the beak,
Now in the waist, the deck, in every cabin,
I flamed amazement. Sometime I'd divide
And burn in many places; on the topmast,
The yards and bowsprit, would I flame distinctly,   200
Then meet and join. Jove's lightning, the precursors
O'th'dreadful thunderclaps, more momentary
And sight out-running were not. The fire and cracks
Of sulphurous roaring the most mighty Neptune
Seem to besiege, and make his bold waves tremble,
Yea, his dread trident shake.

PROSPERO   My brave spirit!
Who was so firm, so constant, that this coil
Would not infect his reason?

ARIEL   Not a soul
But felt a fever of the mad, and played
Some tricks of desperation. All but mariners   210
Plunged in the foaming brine and quit the vessel,
Then all afire with me. The King's son Ferdinand,
With hair up-staring – then like reeds, not hair –
Was the first man that leaped; cried 'Hell is empty,
And all the devils are here!'

PROSPERO   Why, that's my spirit!
But was not this nigh shore?

ARIEL   Close by, my master.

PROSPERO

But are they, Ariel, safe?

ARIEL   Not a hair perished.
On their sustaining garments not a blemish,
But fresher than before; and as thou bad'st me,
In troops I have dispersed them 'bout the isle.   220
The King's son have I landed by himself,

Whom I left cooling of the air with sighs
In an odd angle of the isle, and sitting,
His arms in this sad knot.

PROSPERO   Of the King's ship,
The mariners, say how thou hast disposed,
And all the rest o'th'fleet?

ARIEL   Safely in harbour
Is the King's ship, in the deep nook where once
Thou called'st me up at midnight to fetch dew
From the still-vexed Bermudas, there she's hid;
230 The mariners all under hatches stowed,
Who, with a charm joined to their suffered labour,
I have left asleep. And for the rest o'th'fleet,
Which I dispersed, they all have met again,
And are upon the Mediterranean float
Bound sadly home for Naples,
Supposing that they saw the King's ship wrecked,
And his great person perish.

PROSPERO   Ariel, thy charge
Exactly is performed; but there's more work.
What is the time o'th'day?

ARIEL   Past the mid-season.

PROSPERO
240 At least two glasses. The time 'twixt six and now
Must by us both be spent most preciously.

ARIEL
Is there more toil? Since thou dost give me pains,
Let me remember thee what thou hast promised,
Which is not yet performed me.

PROSPERO   How now? Moody?
What is't thou canst demand?

ARIEL   My liberty.

PROSPERO
Before the time be out? No more.

[handwritten margin note: Naples Italy to believe that their King is dead. all or native?]

ARIEL   I prithee,
Remember I have done thee worthy service,
Told thee no lies, made no mistakings, served
Without or grudge or grumblings. Thou did promise
To bate me a full year.

PROSPERO   Dost thou forget   250
From what a torment I did free thee?

ARIEL   No.

PROSPERO
Thou dost, and think'st it much to tread the ooze
Of the salt deep,
To run upon the sharp wind of the north,
To do me business in the veins o'th'earth
When it is baked with frost.

ARIEL   I do not, sir.

PROSPERO
Thou liest, malignant thing! Hast thou forgot
The foul witch Sycorax, who with age and envy
Was grown into a hoop? Hast thou forgot her?

ARIEL
No, sir.

PROSPERO Thou hast! Where was she born? Speak. Tell
       me!   260

ARIEL
Sir, in Algiers.

PROSPERO   O, was she so? I must
Once in a month recount what thou hast been,
Which thou forget'st. This damned witch Sycorax,
For mischiefs manifold, and sorceries terrible
To enter human hearing, from Algiers,
Thou know'st, was banished; for one thing she did
They would not take her life. Is not this true?

ARIEL
Ay, sir.

PROSPERO
 This blue-eyed hag was hither brought with child,
270 And here was left by th'sailors. Thou my slave,
 As thou report'st thyself, was then her servant;
 And for thou wast a spirit too delicate
 To act her earthy and abhorred commands,
 Refusing her grand hests, she did confine thee,
 By help of her more potent ministers,
 And in her most unmitigable rage,
 Into a cloven pine, within which rift
 Imprisoned thou didst painfully remain
 A dozen years; within which space she died,
280 And left thee there, where thou didst vent thy groans
 As fast as millwheels strike. Then was this island –
 Save for the son that she did litter here,
 A freckled whelp, hag-born – not honoured with
 A human shape.
ARIEL   Yes, Caliban her son.
PROSPERO
 Dull thing, I say so – he, that Caliban
 Whom now I keep in service. Thou best know'st
 What torment I did find thee in. Thy groans
 Did make wolves howl, and penetrate the breasts
 Of ever-angry bears. It was a torment
290 To lay upon the damned, which Sycorax
 Could not again undo. It was mine art,
 When I arrived and heard thee, that made gape
 The pine, and let thee out.
ARIEL   I thank thee, master.
PROSPERO
 If thou more murmur'st, I will rend an oak
 And peg thee in his knotty entrails till
 Thou hast howled away twelve winters.
ARIEL   Pardon, master.

I will be correspondent to command,
And do my spriting gently.
PROSPERO　　　　　　　　　Do so, and after two days
I will discharge thee.
ARIEL　　　　　　　That's my noble master!
What shall I do? Say what! What shall I do?　　　　　300
PROSPERO
Go make thyself like to a nymph o'th'sea;
Be subject to no sight but thine and mine, invisible
To every eyeball else. Go take this shape
And hither come in't. Go! Hence with diligence.
　　　　　　　　　　　　　　　　　Exit Ariel
Awake, dear heart, awake! Thou hast slept well.
Awake.
MIRANDA The strangeness of your story put
Heaviness in me.
PROSPERO　　　　　Shake it off. Come on,
We'll visit Caliban, my slave, who never
Yields us kind answer.
MIRANDA　　　　　　　'Tis a villain, sir,
I do not love to look on.
PROSPERO　　　　　　　But, as 'tis,　　　　　310
We cannot miss him. He does make our fire,
Fetch in our wood, and serves in offices
That profit us. – What ho! Slave! Caliban!
Thou earth, thou! Speak!
CALIBAN (*within*)　　　　There's wood enough within.
PROSPERO
Come forth, I say; there's other business for thee.
Come, thou tortoise, when?
　　　Enter Ariel, like a water-nymph
Fine apparition! My quaint Ariel,
Hark in thine ear. (*He whispers.*)

like his brother, hypocrisy.
his side
~~Caliban Ferm.~~
a dukedom.

ARIEL   My lord, it shall be done.

Exit

PROSPERO

Thou poisonous slave, got by the devil himself
320   Upon thy wicked dam, come forth!

Enter Caliban

CALIBAN

As wicked dew as e'er my mother brush
With raven's feather from unwholesome
Drop on you both! A southwest blow on y
And blister you all o'er!

PROSPERO

For this, be sure, tonight thou shalt have cram
Side-stitches, that shall pen thy breath up; urch
Shall, for that vast of night that they may work
All exercise on thee. Thou shalt be pinched
As thick as honeycomb, each pinch more stinging
Than bees that made 'em.

washing
a lot of
pain in
him.
slaves
a very
nasty
side.

CALIBAN   I must eat my dinner.
330   This island's mine, by Sycorax my mother,
Which thou tak'st from me. When thou cam'st first
Thou strok'st me, and made much of me; wouldst give me
Water with berries in't, and teach me how

Caliban   To name the bigger light, and how the less,
can not   That burn by day and night. And then I loved thee,
understand   And showed thee all the qualities o'th'isle,
why   The fresh springs, brine-pits, barren place and fertile –
Prospero   Cursed be I that did so! All the charms
is like
340   Of Sycorax – toads, beetles, bats – light on you!
this   For I am all the subjects that you have,
to him.   Which first was mine own king; and here you sty me
In this hard rock, whiles you do keep from me
The rest o'th'island.

exploit

PROSPERO   Thou most lying slave,

Political chg: (handwritten)

Whom stripes may move, not kindness! I have used thee,
Filth as thou art, with human care, and lodged thee
In mine own cell, till thou didst seek to violate
The honour of my child.

CALIBAN
O ho, O ho! Would't had been done!
Thou didst prevent me. I had peopled else
This isle with Calibans.

MIRANDA   Abhorrèd slave,
Which any print of goodness wilt not take,
Being capable of all ill! I pitied thee,
Took pains to make thee speak, taught thee each hour
One thing or other. When thou didst not, savage,
Know thine own meaning, but wouldst gabble like
A thing most brutish, I endowed thy purposes
With words that made them known. But thy vile race,
Though thou didst learn, had that in't which good
      natures
Could not abide to be with. Therefore wast thou
Deservedly confined into this rock,
Who hadst deserved more than a prison.

CALIBAN
You taught me language, and my profit on't
Is, I know how to curse. The red plague rid you
For learning me your language!

PROSPERO   Hag-seed, hence!
Fetch us in fuel; and be quick, thou'rt best,
To answer other business. Shrug'st thou, malice?
If thou neglect'st, or dost unwillingly
What I command, I'll rack thee with old cramps,
Fill all thy bones with aches, make thee roar
That beasts shall tremble at thy din.

CALIBAN   No, pray thee.
(*Aside*) I must obey. His art is of such power,

[Handwritten marginal notes:]
Attempted to rape Miranda!
— Would have done if she/Prosp didn't stop him
350
Makes a point that through teaching him things like language she has enough to teach him enough to understand
To overthrow Prospero.
She has suddenly transformed roles with Caliban) She is now lower than him
360
Time a responsibility to educate him
→ Threatening to use his magic
370
Colonialisation
Believes that Prospero is a lot more power- ful than him.

It would control my dam's god Setebos,
And make a vassal of him.

PROSPERO   So, slave, hence!

Exit Caliban

Enter Ferdinand, and Ariel, invisible, playing and
singing

ARIEL   *Song*
          Come unto these yellow sands,
              And then take hands.
          Curtsied when you have, and kissed,
              The wild waves whist.
          Foot it featly here and there,
380   And sweet sprites the burden bear.
                  Hark, hark,
                  The watch-dogs bark.
          (*Burden, dispersedly*) Bow-wow, bow-wow!
                  Hark, hark, I hear
              The strain of strutting chanticleer
              Cry cock-a-diddle-dow!

FERDINAND
          Where should this music be? I'th'air, or th'earth?
          It sounds no more; and sure it waits upon
          Some god o'th'island. Sitting on a bank,
390   Weeping again the King my father's wreck,
          This music crept by me upon the waters,
          Allaying both their fury and my passion
          With its sweet air. Thence I have followed it,
          Or it hath drawn me rather; but 'tis gone.
          No, it begins again.

ARIEL   *Song*
          Full fathom five thy father lies,
          Of his bones are coral made;
          Those are pearls that were his eyes;
          Nothing of him that doth fade

But doth suffer a sea-change   400
Into something rich and strange.
Sea-nymphs hourly ring his knell.
Hark, now I hear them, ding dong bell.

(*Burden*)   Ding, dong.

FERDINAND

The ditty does remember my drowned father.
This is no mortal business, nor no sound
That the earth owes. I hear it now above me.

PROSPERO (*to Miranda*)

The fringèd curtains of thine eye advance,
And say what thou seest yond.

MIRANDA   What is't? A spirit?
Lord, how it looks about! Believe me, sir,
It carries a brave form. But 'tis a spirit.

PROSPERO

No, wench, it eats and sleeps, and hath such senses
As we have, such. This gallant which thou seest
Was in the wreck; and, but he's something stained
With grief – that's beauty's canker – thou mightst call
   him
A goodly person. He hath lost his fellows,
And strays about to find 'em.

MIRANDA   I might call him
A thing divine, for nothing natural
I ever saw so noble.

PROSPERO (*aside*)   It goes on, I see,
As my soul prompts it. (*To Ariel*) Spirit, fine spirit, I'll
   free thee   420
Within two days for this.

FERDINAND (*to Miranda*)   Most sure, the goddess
On whom these airs attend! Vouchsafe my prayer
May know if you remain upon this island,
And that you will some good instruction give

How I may bear me here. My prime request,
Which I do last pronounce, is – O you wonder! –
If you be <u>maid or no</u>?

MIRANDA   No wonder, sir,
But certainly a maid.

FERDINAND   My language? Heavens!
I am the best of them that speak this speech,
430   Were I but where 'tis spoken.

PROSPERO   How, the best?
What wert thou if the King of Naples heard thee?

FERDINAND
A single thing, as I am now, that wonders
To hear thee speak of Naples. He does hear me,
And that he does, I weep. Myself am Naples,
Who with mine eyes, never since at ebb, beheld
The King my father wrecked.

MIRANDA   Alack, for mercy!

FERDINAND
Yes, faith, and all his lords, the Duke of Milan
And his brave son being twain.

PROSPERO (aside)   The Duke of Milan
And his more braver daughter could control thee,
440   If now 'twere fit to do't. At the first sight
They have changed eyes. Delicate Ariel,
I'll set thee free for this. – A word, good sir.
I fear you have done yourself some wrong; a word.

MIRANDA
Why speaks my father so ungently? This
Is the third man that e'er I saw, the first
That e'er I sighed for. Pity move my father
To be inclined my way.

FERDINAND   O, if a virgin,
And your affection not gone forth, I'll make you
The Queen of Naples.

PROSPERO   Soft, sir, one word more!
  (*Aside*) They are both in either's powers; but this swift
      business   450
  I must uneasy make, lest too light winning
  Make the prize light. – One word more! I charge thee
  That thou attend me. Thou dost here usurp
  The name thou ow'st not, and hast put thyself
  Upon this island as a spy, to win it
  From me, the lord on't.
FERDINAND   No, as I am a man!
MIRANDA
  There's nothing ill can dwell in such a temple.
  If the ill spirit have so fair a house,
  Good things will strive to dwell with't.
PROSPERO   Follow me.
  (*To Miranda*) Speak not you for him; he's a traitor. –
      Come!
  I'll manacle thy neck and feet together;   460
  Sea water shalt thou drink; thy food shall be
  The fresh-brook mussels, withered roots, and husks
  Wherein the acorn cradled. Follow.
FERDINAND   No!
  I will resist such entertainment till
  Mine enemy has more power.
      He draws his sword, and is charmed from moving
MIRANDA   O dear father,
  Make not too rash a trial of him, for
  He's gentle, and not fearful.
PROSPERO   What, I say,
  My foot my tutor? Put thy sword up, traitor,
  Who mak'st a show but dar'st not strike, thy conscience   470
  Is so possessed with guilt. Come from thy ward,
  For I can here disarm thee with this stick,
  And make thy weapon drop.

MIRANDA   Beseech you, father!

PROSPERO
Hence! Hang not on my garments.

MIRANDA   Sir, have pity.
I'll be his surety.

PROSPERO   Silence! One word more
Shall make me chide thee, if not hate thee. What,
An advocate for an impostor? Hush!
Thou think'st there is no more such shapes as he,
Having seen but him and Caliban. Foolish wench,
480   To th'most of men this is a Caliban,
And they to him are angels.

MIRANDA   My affections
Are then most humble. I have no ambition
To see a goodlier man.

PROSPERO (*to Ferdinand*) Come on, obey.
Thy nerves are in their infancy again,
And have no vigour in them.

FERDINAND   So they are.
My spirits, as in a dream, are all bound up.
My father's loss, the weakness which I feel,
The wreck of all my friends, nor this man's threats
To whom I am subdued, are but light to me,
490   Might I but through my prison once a day
Behold this maid. All corners else o'th'earth
Let liberty make use of; space enough
Have I in such a prison.

PROSPERO (*aside*)   It works. (*To Ferdinand*) Come
on!
(*To Ariel*) Thou hast done well, fine Ariel. (*To
Ferdinand*) Follow me.
(*To Ariel*) Hark what thou else shalt do me.

MIRANDA   Be of comfort.
My father's of a better nature, sir,

He seems to have lost everything and everything is scarier because of [handwritten marginal note]

Than he appears by speech. This is unwonted
Which now came from him.

PROSPERO (*to Ariel*)   Thou shalt be as free
As mountain winds; but then exactly do
All points of my command.

ARIEL   To th'syllable.   500

PROSPERO

Come, follow! (*To Miranda*) Speak not for him.

Exeunt

*

Enter Alonso, Sebastian, Antonio, Gonzalo, Adrian,   II.I
Francisco, and others

GONZALO (*to Alonso*)

Beseech you, sir, be merry. You have cause –
So have we all – of joy, for our escape
Is much beyond our loss. Our hint of woe
Is common; every day some sailor's wife,
The masters of some merchant, and the merchant
Have just our theme of woe. But for the miracle,
I mean our preservation, few in millions
Can speak like us. Then wisely, good sir, weigh
Our sorrow with our comfort.

ALONSO   Prithee, peace.

SEBASTIAN (*aside to Antonio*) He receives comfort like   10
cold porridge.

ANTONIO (*aside to Sebastian*) The visitor will not give
him o'er so.

SEBASTIAN (*aside to Antonio*) Look, he's winding up the
watch of his wit. By and by it will strike.

GONZALO Sir, –

SEBASTIAN One: tell.

GONZALO – when every grief is entertained that's offered, comes to th'entertainer –

20 SEBASTIAN A dollar.

GONZALO Dolour comes to him indeed. You have spoken truer than you purposed.

SEBASTIAN You have taken it wiselier than I meant you should.

GONZALO (*to Alonso*) Therefore, my lord –

ANTONIO Fie, what a spendthrift is he of his tongue!

ALONSO (*to Gonzalo*) I prithee, spare.

GONZALO Well, I have done. But yet –

SEBASTIAN He will be talking.

30 ANTONIO Which of he or Adrian, for a good wager, first begins to crow?

SEBASTIAN The old cock.

ANTONIO The cockerel.

SEBASTIAN Done. The wager?

ANTONIO A laughter.

SEBASTIAN A match.

ADRIAN Though this island seem to be desert –

ANTONIO Ha, ha, ha!

SEBASTIAN So, you're paid.

40 ADRIAN Uninhabitable, and almost inaccessible –

SEBASTIAN Yet –

ADRIAN Yet –

ANTONIO He could not miss't.

ADRIAN It must needs be of subtle, tender, and delicate temperance.

ANTONIO Temperance was a delicate wench.

SEBASTIAN Ay, and a subtle, as he most learnedly delivered.

ADRIAN The air breathes upon us here most sweetly.

50 SEBASTIAN As if it had lungs, and rotten ones.

ANTONIO Or as 'twere perfumed by a fen.

GONZALO Here is everything advantageous to life.

ANTONIO True, save means to live.

SEBASTIAN Of that there's none, or little.

GONZALO How lush and lusty the grass looks! How green!

ANTONIO The ground, indeed, is tawny.

SEBASTIAN With an eye of green in't.

ANTONIO He misses not much.

SEBASTIAN No, he doth but mistake the truth totally.

GONZALO But the rarity of it is, which is, indeed, almost   60
beyond credit –

SEBASTIAN As many vouched rarities are.

GONZALO – that our garments, being, as they were,
drenched in the sea, hold notwithstanding their fresh-
ness and gloss, being rather new-dyed than stained with
salt water.

ANTONIO If but one of his pockets could speak, would it
not say he lies?

SEBASTIAN Ay, or very falsely pocket up his report.

GONZALO Methinks our garments are now as fresh as when   70
we put them on first in Afric, at the marriage of the
King's fair daughter Claribel to the King of Tunis.

SEBASTIAN 'Twas a sweet marriage, and we prosper well
in our return.

ADRIAN Tunis was never graced before with such a
paragon to their queen.

GONZALO Not since widow Dido's time.

ANTONIO Widow? A pox o'that! How came that 'widow'
in? Widow Dido!

SEBASTIAN What if he had said 'widower Aeneas' too?   80
Good lord, how you take it!

ADRIAN (*to Gonzalo*) 'Widow Dido', said you? You make
me study of that. She was of Carthage, not of Tunis.

GONZALO This Tunis, sir, was Carthage.

ADRIAN Carthage?

GONZALO I assure you, Carthage.

ANTONIO His word is more than the miraculous harp.

SEBASTIAN He hath raised the wall, and houses too.

ANTONIO What impossible matter will he make easy next?

90 SEBASTIAN I think he will carry this island home in his pocket, and give it his son for an apple.

ANTONIO And sowing the kernels of it in the sea, bring forth more islands.

GONZALO Ay –

ANTONIO Why, in good time.

GONZALO (*to Alonso*) Sir, we were talking that our garments seem now as fresh as when we were at Tunis at the marriage of your daughter, who is now Queen.

ANTONIO And the rarest that e'er came there.

100 SEBASTIAN Bate, I beseech you, widow Dido.

ANTONIO O, widow Dido? Ay, widow Dido.

GONZALO Is not, sir, my doublet as fresh as the first day I wore it? I mean, in a sort –

ANTONIO That sort was well fished for.

GONZALO – when I wore it at your daughter's marriage.

ALONSO
You cram these words into mine ears against
The stomach of my sense. Would I had never
Married my daughter there! For, coming thence,
My son is lost, and, in my rate, she too,
110 Who is so far from Italy removed
I ne'er again shall see her. O thou mine heir
Of Naples and of Milan, what strange fish
Hath made his meal on thee?

FRANCISCO   Sir, he may live.
I saw him beat the surges under him,
And ride upon their backs. He trod the water,
Whose enmity he flung aside, and breasted
The surge most swoll'n that met him. His bold head

'Bove the contentious waves he kept, and oared
Himself with his good arms in lusty stroke
To th'shore, that o'er his wave-worn basis bowed,   120
As stooping to relieve him. I not doubt
He came alive to land.

ALONSO   No, no, he's gone.

SEBASTIAN
Sir, you may thank yourself for this great loss,
That would not bless our Europe with your daughter,
But rather loose her to an African,
Where she, at least, is banished from your eye,
Who hath cause to wet the grief on't.

ALONSO   Prithee, peace.

SEBASTIAN
You were kneeled to and importuned otherwise
By all of us, and the fair soul herself
Weighed between loathness and obedience at   130
Which end o'th'beam should bow. We have lost your son,
I fear, for ever. Milan and Naples have
More widows in them of this business' making
Than we bring men to comfort them.
The fault's your own.

ALONSO   So is the dear'st o'th'loss.

GONZALO
My Lord Sebastian,
The truth you speak doth lack some gentleness,
And time to speak it in. You rub the sore,
When you should bring the plaster.

SEBASTIAN   Very well.

ANTONIO And most chirurgeonly!   140

GONZALO (to Alonso)
It is foul weather in us all, good sir,
When you are cloudy.

SEBASTIAN   Foul weather?

ANTONIO   Very foul.

GONZALO

  Had I plantation of this isle, my lord –

ANTONIO

  He'd sow't with nettle-seed.

SEBASTIAN   Or docks, or mallows.

GONZALO

  And were the king on't, what would I do?

SEBASTIAN 'Scape being drunk, for want of wine.

GONZALO

  I'th'commonwealth I would by contraries

  Execute all things. For no kind of traffic

  Would I admit; no name of magistrate;

150 Letters should not be known; riches, poverty,

  And use of service, none; contract, succession,

  Bourn, bound of land, tilth, vineyard, none;

  No use of metal, corn, or wine, or oil;

  No occupation, all men idle, all;

  And women too, but innocent and pure;

  No sovereignty –

SEBASTIAN   Yet he would be king on't.

ANTONIO The latter end of his commonwealth forgets
  the beginning.

GONZALO

  All things in common nature should produce

160 Without sweat or endeavour. Treason, felony,

  Sword, pike, knife, gun, or need of any engine

  Would I not have; but nature should bring forth

  Of it own kind all foison, all abundance,

  To feed my innocent people.

SEBASTIAN No marrying 'mong his subjects?

ANTONIO None, man, all idle – whores and knaves.

GONZALO

  I would with such perfection govern, sir,

T'excel the Golden Age.

SEBASTIAN   'Save his majesty!

ANTONIO

Long live Gonzalo!

GONZALO   And – do you mark me, sir?

ALONSO

Prithee, no more. Thou dost talk nothing to me.   170

GONZALO I do well believe your highness, and did it to
minister occasion to these gentlemen, who are of such
sensible and nimble lungs that they always use to laugh
at nothing.

ANTONIO 'Twas you we laughed at.

GONZALO Who, in this kind of merry fooling, am nothing
to you; so you may continue, and laugh at nothing still.

ANTONIO What a blow was there given!

SEBASTIAN An it had not fallen flat-long.

GONZALO You are gentlemen of brave mettle. You would   180
lift the moon out of her sphere, if she would continue
in it five weeks without changing.

Enter Ariel, playing solemn music

SEBASTIAN We would so, and then go a-bat-fowling.

ANTONIO Nay, good my lord, be not angry.

GONZALO No, I warrant you, I will not adventure my
discretion so weakly. Will you laugh me asleep, for I
am very heavy?

ANTONIO Go sleep, and hear us.

All sleep, except Alonso, Sebastian, and Antonio

ALONSO

What, all so soon asleep? I wish mine eyes

Would with themselves shut up my thoughts. I find   190

They are inclined to do so.

SEBASTIAN   Please you, sir,

Do not omit the heavy offer of it.

It seldom visits sorrow; when it doth,
It is a comforter.

ANTONIO   We two, my lord,
Will guard your person while you take your rest,
And watch your safety.

ALONSO   Thank you. Wondrous heavy.
    Alonso sleeps.   *Exit Ariel*

SEBASTIAN
What a strange drowsiness possesses them!

ANTONIO
It is the quality o'th'climate.

SEBASTIAN   Why
Doth it not then our eyelids sink? I find
Not myself disposed to sleep.

ANTONIO
Nor I; my spirits are nimble.
They fell together all, as by consent;
They dropped, as by a thunderstroke. What might,
Worthy Sebastian, O, what might? – No more!
And yet methinks I see it in thy face,
What thou shouldst be. Th'occasion speaks thee, and
My strong imagination sees a crown
Dropping upon thy head.

SEBASTIAN   What, art thou waking?

ANTONIO
Do you not hear me speak?

SEBASTIAN   I do, and surely
It is a sleepy language, and thou speak'st
Out of thy sleep. What is it thou didst say?
This is a strange repose, to be asleep
With eyes wide open – standing, speaking, moving,
And yet so fast asleep.

ANTONIO   Noble Sebastian,
Thou let'st thy fortune sleep – die, rather; wink'st

Whiles thou art waking.

SEBASTIAN   Thou dost snore distinctly.
There's meaning in thy snores.

ANTONIO
I am more serious than my custom. You
Must be so too, if heed me; which to do,
Trebles thee o'er.

SEBASTIAN   Well, I am standing water.   220

ANTONIO
I'll teach you how to flow.

SEBASTIAN   Do so. To ebb
Hereditary sloth instructs me.

ANTONIO   O,
If you but knew how you the purpose cherish
Whiles thus you mock it; how in stripping it,
You more invest it! Ebbing men, indeed,
Most often, do so near the bottom run
By their own fear or sloth.

SEBASTIAN   Prithee, say on.
The setting of thine eye and cheek proclaim
A matter from thee; and a birth, indeed,
Which throes thee much to yield.

ANTONIO   Thus, sir: 230
Although this lord of weak remembrance, this,
Who shall be of as little memory
When he is earthed, hath here almost persuaded –
For he's a spirit of persuasion, only
Professes to persuade – the King his son's alive,
'Tis as impossible that he's undrowned
As he that sleeps here swims.

SEBASTIAN   I have no hope
That he's undrowned.

ANTONIO   O, out of that 'no hope'
What great hope have you! No hope that way, is

240   Another way so high a hope that even
        Ambition cannot pierce a wink beyond,
        But doubt discovery there. Will you grant with me
        That Ferdinand is drowned?

SEBASTIAN   He's gone.

ANTONIO   Then tell me,
        Who's the next heir of Naples?

SEBASTIAN   Claribel.

ANTONIO
        She that is Queen of Tunis; she that dwells
        Ten leagues beyond man's life; she that from Naples
        Can have no note, unless the sun were post –
        The man i'th'moon's too slow – till newborn chins
        Be rough and razorable; she that from whom
250   We all were sea-swallowed, though some cast again,
        And by that destiny to perform an act
        Whereof what's past is prologue, what to come
        In yours and my discharge.

SEBASTIAN
        What stuff is this? How say you?
        'Tis true my brother's daughter's Queen of Tunis,
        So is she heir of Naples, 'twixt which regions
        There is some space.

ANTONIO   A space whose every cubit
        Seems to cry out, 'How shall that Claribel
        Measure us back to Naples? Keep in Tunis,
260   And let Sebastian wake.' Say this were death
        That now hath seized them, why, they were no worse
        Than now they are. There be that can rule Naples
        As well as he that sleeps; lords that can prate
        As amply and unnecessarily
        As this Gonzalo – I myself could make
        A chough of as deep chat. O, that you bore
        The mind that I do! What a sleep were this

For your advancement! Do you understand me?

SEBASTIAN
Methinks I do.

ANTONIO   And how does your content
Tender your own good fortune?

SEBASTIAN   I remember   270
You did supplant your brother Prospero.

ANTONIO   True:
And look how well my garments sit upon me,
Much feater than before. My brother's servants
Were then my fellows; now they are my men.

SEBASTIAN
But for your conscience?

ANTONIO
Ay, sir, where lies that? If 'twere a kibe,
'Twould put me to my slipper, but I feel not
This deity in my bosom. Twenty consciences
That stand 'twixt me and Milan, candied be they,
And melt ere they molest. Here lies your brother,   280
No better than the earth he lies upon;
If he were that which now he's like – that's dead –
Whom I with this obedient steel, three inches of it,
Can lay to bed for ever; whiles you, doing thus,
To the perpetual wink for aye might put
This ancient morsel, this Sir Prudence, who
Should not upbraid our course. For all the rest,
They'll take suggestion as a cat laps milk;
They'll tell the clock to any business that
We say befits the hour.

SEBASTIAN   Thy case, dear friend,   290
Shall be my precedent. As thou got'st Milan,
I'll come by Naples. Draw thy sword. One stroke
Shall free thee from the tribute which thou payest,
And I the King shall love thee.

ANTONIO   Draw together,
  And when I rear my hand, do you the like
  To fall it on Gonzalo.
SEBASTIAN   O, but one word.
      Enter Ariel with music
ARIEL
  My master through his art foresees the danger
  That you, his friend, are in, and sends me forth –
  For else his project dies – to keep them living.
      Sings in Gonzalo's ear
300   While you here do snoring lie,
                    Open-eyed conspiracy
                          His time doth take.
                    If of life you keep a care,
                    Shake off slumber and beware.
                          Awake, awake!
ANTONIO
  Then let us both be sudden.
GONZALO (*waking*)
  Now, good angels preserve the King!
      He shakes Alonso. The others awake
ALONSO
  Why, how now, ho! Awake? Why are you drawn?
  Wherefore this ghastly looking?
GONZALO   What's the matter?
SEBASTIAN
310 Whiles we stood here securing your repose,
  Even now, we heard a hollow burst of bellowing
  Like bulls, or rather lions. Did't not wake you?
  It struck mine ear most terribly.
ALONSO   I heard nothing.
ANTONIO
  O, 'twas a din to fright a monster's ear,
  To make an earthquake. Sure it was the roar

Of a whole herd of lions.

ALONSO   Heard you this, Gonzalo?

GONZALO

Upon mine honour, sir, I heard a humming,
And that a strange one too, which did awake me.
I shaked you, sir, and cried. As mine eyes opened,
I saw their weapons drawn. There was a noise,   320
That's verily. 'Tis best we stand upon our guard,
Or that we quit this place. Let's draw our weapons.

ALONSO

Lead off this ground, and let's make further search
For my poor son.

GONZALO   Heavens keep him from these beasts!
For he is sure i'th'island.

ALONSO   Lead away.

ARIEL

Prospero my lord shall know what I have done.
So, King, go safely on to seek thy son.   *Exeunt*

Enter Caliban, with a burden of wood. A noise of   II.2
thunder heard

CALIBAN

All the infections that the sun sucks up
From bogs, fens, flats, on Prosper fall, and make him
By inch-meal a disease! His spirits hear me,
And yet I needs must curse. But they'll nor pinch,
Fright me with urchin-shows, pitch me i'th'mire,
Nor lead me like a firebrand in the dark
Out of my way, unless he bid 'em. But
For every trifle are they set upon me:
Sometime like apes, that mow and chatter at me,
And after bite me; then like hedgehogs, which   10
Lie tumbling in my barefoot way, and mount

Their pricks at my footfall; sometime am I
All wound with adders, who with cloven tongues
Do hiss me into madness.
> *Enter Trinculo*

                              Lo, now lo!
Here comes a spirit of his, and to torment me
For bringing wood in slowly. I'll fall flat.
Perchance he will not mind me.
> *He lies down and covers himself with a cloak*

TRINCULO Here's neither bush nor shrub to bear off any
weather at all, and another storm brewing – I hear it
sing i'th'wind. Yond same black cloud, yond huge one,
looks like a foul bombard that would shed his liquor.
If it should thunder as it did before, I know not where
to hide my head. Yond same cloud cannot choose but
fall by pailfuls. (*He sees Caliban.*) What have we here?
A man or a fish? Dead or alive? A fish: he smells like
a fish; a very ancient and fish-like smell, a kind of not-
of-the-newest poor-John. A strange fish! Were I in
England now – as once I was – and had but this fish
painted, not a holiday fool there but would give a piece
of silver. There would this monster make a man; any
strange beast there makes a man. When they will not
give a doit to relieve a lame beggar, they will lay out
ten to see a dead Indian. Legged like a man, and his
fins like arms! Warm, o'my troth! I do now let loose
my opinion, hold it no longer. This is no fish, but an
islander that hath lately suffered by a thunderbolt.
> *Thunder*

Alas, the storm is come again. My best way is to
creep under his gaberdine. There is no other shelter
hereabout. Misery acquaints a man with strange bedfellows! I will here shroud till the dregs of the storm be
past.

Trinculo hides under the cloak. Enter Stephano, singing,
with a bottle

STEPHANO

> I shall no more to sea, to sea,
>   Here shall I die ashore –

This is a very scurvy tune to sing at a man's funeral.
Well, here's my comfort.

He drinks, then sings

> The master, the swabber, the boatswain and I,
>   The gunner and his mate,
> Loved Mall, Meg, and Marian, and Margery,
>   But none of us cared for Kate.
>   For she had a tongue with a tang,   50
>   Would cry to a sailor, 'Go hang!'
> She loved not the savour of tar nor of pitch,
> Yet a tailor might scratch her where'er she did itch.
>   Then to sea, boys, and let her go hang!

This is a scurvy tune too, but here's my comfort.

He drinks

CALIBAN Do not torment me! O!

STEPHANO What's the matter? Have we devils here? Do
you put tricks upon's with savages and men of Ind?
Ha? I have not 'scaped drowning to be afeard now of
your four legs. For it hath been said, 'As proper a man   60
as ever went on four legs cannot make him give ground';
and it shall be said so again, while Stephano breathes
at' nostrils.

CALIBAN The spirit torments me! O!

STEPHANO This is some monster of the isle with four legs,
who hath got, as I take it, an ague. Where the devil
should he learn our language? I will give him some
relief, if it be but for that. If I can recover him and keep
him tame, and get to Naples with him, he's a present
for any emperor that ever trod on neat's leather.   70

CALIBAN Do not torment me, prithee! I'll bring my wood home faster.

STEPHANO He's in his fit now, and does not talk after the wisest. He shall taste of my bottle. If he have never drunk wine afore, it will go near to remove his fit. If I can recover him and keep him tame, I will not take too much for him. He shall pay for him that hath him, and that soundly.

CALIBAN Thou dost me yet but little hurt. Thou wilt anon,
80 I know it by thy trembling. Now Prosper works upon thee.

STEPHANO Come on your ways. Open your mouth. Here is that which will give language to you, cat. Open your mouth. This will shake your shaking, I can tell you, and that soundly. (*He gives Caliban wine, Caliban spits it out.*) You cannot tell who's your friend. Open your chops again.

TRINCULO I should know that voice. It should be – but he is drowned, and these are devils. O, defend me!

90 STEPHANO Four legs and two voices – a most delicate monster! His forward voice now is to speak well of his friend; his backward voice is to utter foul speeches, and to detract. If all the wine in my bottle will recover him, I will help his ague. Come! (*Caliban drinks.*) Amen! I will pour some in thy other mouth.

TRINCULO Stephano!

STEPHANO Doth thy other mouth call me? Mercy, mercy! This is a devil, and no monster. I will leave him, I have no long spoon.

100 TRINCULO Stephano? If thou beest Stephano, touch me and speak to me, for I am Trinculo – be not afeared – thy good friend Trinculo.

STEPHANO If thou beest Trinculo, come forth. I'll pull thee by the lesser legs. If any be Trinculo's legs, these

are they. (*He pulls Trinculo out.*) Thou art very Trinculo
indeed! How cam'st thou to be the siege of this mooncalf? Can he vent Trinculos?

TRINCULO I took him to be killed with a thunder-stroke.
But art thou not drowned, Stephano? I hope now thou
art not drowned. Is the storm overblown? I hid me   110
under the dead mooncalf's gaberdine for fear of the
storm. And art thou living, Stephano? O Stephano, two
Neapolitans 'scaped!

STEPHANO Prithee, do not turn me about, my stomach is
not constant.

CALIBAN These be fine things, an if they be not sprites.
That's a brave god, and bears celestial liquor. I will
kneel to him.

STEPHANO How didst thou 'scape? How cam'st thou
hither? Swear by this bottle how thou cam'st hither.   120
I escaped upon a butt of sack which the sailors heaved
o'erboard, by this bottle – which I made of the bark
of a tree, with mine own hands, since I was cast
ashore.

CALIBAN I'll swear upon that bottle to be thy true subject,
for the liquor is not earthly.

STEPHANO Hear, swear then how thou escap'dst.

TRINCULO Swum ashore, man, like a duck. I can swim
like a duck, I'll be sworn.

STEPHANO Here, kiss the book. (*Trinculo drinks.*) Though   130
thou canst swim like a duck, thou art made like a goose.

TRINCULO O Stephano, hast any more of this?

STEPHANO The whole butt, man. My cellar is in a rock
by th'seaside, where my wine is hid. How now, mooncalf? How does thine ague?

CALIBAN Hast thou not dropped from heaven?

STEPHANO Out o'th'moon, I do assure thee. I was the
Man i'th'Moon, when time was.

CALIBAN I have seen thee in her, and I do adore thee. My
140   mistress showed me thee, and thy dog, and thy bush.

STEPHANO Come, swear to that. Kiss the book. I will
       furnish it anon with new contents. Swear! (*Caliban
       drinks.*)

TRINCULO By this good light, this is a very shallow
       monster! I afeard of him? A very weak monster! The
       Man i'th'Moon? A most poor credulous monster! – Well
       drawn, monster, in good sooth!

CALIBAN I'll show thee every fertile inch o'th'island, and
       I will kiss thy foot. I prithee, be my god.

150 TRINCULO By this light, a most perfidious and drunken
       monster! When's god's asleep, he'll rob his bottle.

CALIBAN I'll kiss thy foot. I'll swear myself thy subject.

STEPHANO Come on then, down and swear.

TRINCULO I shall laugh myself to death at this puppy-
       headed monster! A most scurvy monster! I could find
       in my heart to beat him –

STEPHANO Come, kiss.

TRINCULO – but that the poor monster's in drink. An
       abominable monster!

CALIBAN
160   I'll show thee the best springs. I'll pluck thee berries.
       I'll fish for thee, and get thee wood enough.
       A plague upon the tyrant that I serve!
       I'll bear him no more sticks, but follow thee,
       Thou wondrous man.

TRINCULO A most ridiculous monster, to make a wonder
       of a poor drunkard!

CALIBAN
       I prithee, let me bring thee where crabs grow;
       And I with my long nails will dig thee pignuts,
       Show thee a jay's nest, and instruct thee how
170   To snare the nimble marmoset. I'll bring thee

To clust'ring filberts, and sometimes I'll get thee
Young scamels from the rock. Wilt thou go with me?
STEPHANO I prithee now lead the way without any more
talking. – Trinculo, the King and all our company else
being drowned, we will inherit here. (*To Caliban*) Here,
bear my bottle. – Fellow Trinculo, we'll fill him by and
by again.
CALIBAN (*sings drunkenly*)
        Farewell, master! Farewell, farewell!
TRINCULO A howling monster! A drunken monster!
CALIBAN
        No more dams I'll make for fish,   180
        Nor fetch in firing at requiring,
        Nor scrape trencher, nor wash dish.
            Ban, ban, Ca-Caliban,
        Has a new master, get a new man!
Freedom, high-day! High-day, freedom! Freedom,
high-day, freedom!
STEPHANO O brave monster! Lead the way.   *Exeunt*

                    *

Enter Ferdinand, bearing a log   III.1
FERDINAND
There be some sports are painful, and their labour
Delight in them sets off. Some kinds of baseness
Are nobly undergone, and most poor matters
Point to rich ends. This my mean task
Would be as heavy to me as odious, but
The mistress which I serve quickens what's dead,
And makes my labours pleasures. O she is
Ten times more gentle than her father's crabbed,
And he's composed of harshness. I must remove

10   Some thousands of these logs and pile them up,
        Upon a sore injunction. My sweet mistress
        Weeps when she sees me work, and says such baseness
        Had never like executor. I forget;
        But these sweet thoughts do even refresh my labours,
        Most busy, least when I do it.

        Enter Miranda, and Prospero following at a distance

        MIRANDA   Alas, now pray you
        Work not so hard. I would the lightning had
        Burnt up those logs that you are enjoined to pile!
        Pray set it down, and rest you. When this burns,
        'Twill weep for having wearied you. My father
20   Is hard at study. Pray now, rest yourself;   *Magic*
        He's safe for these three hours.   *Books.*

        FERDINAND   O most dear mistress,
        The sun will set before I shall discharge
        What I must strive to do.

        MIRANDA   If you'll sit down,
Tease   I'll bear your logs the while. Pray give me that;
          I'll carry it to the pile.

        FERDINAND   No, precious creature.
        I had rather crack my sinews, break my back,
Very   Than you should such dishonour undergo
Serious While I sit lazy by.

        MIRANDA   It would become me
        As well as it does you; and I should do it
30   With much more ease, for my good will is to it,
        And yours it is against.

        PROSPERO (*aside*)   Poor worm, thou art infected!
        This visitation shows it.

        MIRANDA   You look wearily.

        FERDINAND
        No, noble mistress, 'tis fresh morning with me
        When you are by at night. I do beseech you –

Chiefly that I might set it in my prayers –
What is your name?

MIRANDA   Miranda. – O my father,
I have broke your hest to say so.

FERDINAND   Admired Miranda!
Indeed the top of admiration, worth
What's dearest to the world! Full many a lady
I have eyed with best regard, and many a time   40
Th'harmony of their tongues hath into bondage
Brought my too diligent ear. For several virtues
Have I liked several women; never any
With so full soul but some defect in her
Did quarrel with the noblest grace she owed,
And put it to the foil. But you, O you,
So perfect and so peerless, are created
Of every creature's best.

MIRANDA   I do not know
One of my sex; no woman's face remember,
Save from my glass, mine own. Nor have I seen
More that I may call men than you, good friend,
And my dear father. How features are abroad
I am skilless of; but by my modesty,
The jewel in my dower, I would not wish
Any companion in the world but you,
Nor can imagination form a shape
Besides yourself, to like of. But I prattle
Something too wildly, and my father's precepts
I therein do forget.

FERDINAND   I am in my condition
A prince, Miranda; I do think, a king –   60
I would not so – and would no more endure
This wooden slavery than to suffer
The flesh-fly blow my mouth. Hear my soul speak.
The very instant that I saw you did

My heart fly to your service; there resides
To make me slave to it, and for your sake
Am I this patient log-man.

MIRANDA   Do you love me?

FERDINAND

O heaven, O earth, bear witness to this sound,
And crown what I profess with kind event
70   If I speak true; if hollowly, invert
What best is boded me to mischief! I,
Beyond all limit of what else i'th'world,
Do love, prize, honour you.

MIRANDA   I am a fool
To weep at what I am glad of.

PROSPERO (*aside*)   Fair encounter
Of two most rare affections! Heavens rain grace
On that which breeds between 'em.

FERDINAND   Wherefore weep you?

MIRANDA

At mine unworthiness, that dare not offer
What I desire to give, and much less take
What I shall die to want. But this is trifling,
80   And all the more it seeks to hide itself,
The bigger bulk it shows. Hence, bashful cunning,
And prompt me, plain and holy innocence.
I am your wife, if you will marry me;
If not, I'll die your maid. To be your fellow
You may deny me, but I'll be your servant
Whether you will or no.

FERDINAND (*kneels*)   My mistress, dearest,
And I thus humble ever.

MIRANDA

My husband then?

FERDINAND   Ay, with a heart as willing
As bondage e'er of freedom. Here's my hand.

MIRANDA

And mine, with my heart in't; and now farewell   90
Till half an hour hence.

FERDINAND   A thousand thousand!

Exeunt Ferdinand and Miranda, in different directions

PROSPERO

So glad of this as they I cannot be,
Who are surprised withal, but my rejoicing
At nothing can be more. I'll to my book,
For yet ere suppertime must I perform
Much business appertaining.   *Exit*

Enter Caliban, Stephano, and Trinculo   III.2

STEPHANO Tell not me! When the butt is out we will drink
water, not a drop before; therefore bear up, and board
'em. Servant monster, drink to me.

TRINCULO Servant monster? The folly of this island!
They say there's but five upon this isle. We are three
of them – if th'other two be brained like us, the state
totters.

STEPHANO Drink, servant monster, when I bid thee. Thy
eyes are almost set in thy head.

TRINCULO Where should they be set else? He were a brave   10
monster indeed if they were set in his tail.

STEPHANO My man-monster hath drowned his tongue in
sack. For my part, the sea cannot drown me. I swam,
ere I could recover the shore, five and thirty leagues
off and on. By this light, thou shalt be my lieutenant,
monster, or my standard.

TRINCULO Your lieutenant, if you list; he's no standard.

STEPHANO We'll not run, Monsieur Monster.

TRINCULO Nor go, neither; but you'll lie like dogs, and
yet say nothing neither.   20

STEPHANO Mooncalf, speak once in thy life, if thou beest
    a good mooncalf.

CALIBAN How does thy honour? Let me lick thy shoe. I'll
    not serve him, he is not valiant.

TRINCULO Thou liest, most ignorant monster! I am in case
    to jostle a constable. Why, thou debauched fish thou,
    was there ever man a coward that hath drunk so much
    sack as I today? Wilt thou tell a monstrous lie, being
    but half a fish and half a monster?

30 CALIBAN Lo, how he mocks me! Wilt thou let him, my lord?

TRINCULO 'Lord', quoth he? That a monster should be
    such a natural!

CALIBAN Lo, lo, again! Bite him to death, I prithee.

STEPHANO Trinculo, keep a good tongue in your head. If
    you prove a mutineer, the next tree! The poor monster's
    my subject, and he shall not suffer indignity.

CALIBAN I thank my noble lord. Wilt thou be pleased to
    hearken once again to the suit I made to thee?

STEPHANO Marry, will I. Kneel, and repeat it. I will stand,
40   and so shall Trinculo.

    Enter Ariel, invisible

CALIBAN As I told thee before, I am subject to a tyrant, a
    sorcerer, that by his cunning hath cheated me of the
    island.

ARIEL Thou liest.

CALIBAN (*to Trinculo*) Thou liest, thou jesting monkey
    thou! I would my valiant master would destroy thee. I
    do not lie.

STEPHANO Trinculo, if you trouble him any more in's
    tale, by this hand, I will supplant some of your teeth.

50 TRINCULO Why, I said nothing.

STEPHANO Mum, then, and no more. – Proceed.

CALIBAN
    I say by sorcery he got this isle;

From me he got it. If thy greatness will
Revenge it on him – for I know thou dar'st,
But this thing dare not –

STEPHANO That's most certain.

CALIBAN
Thou shalt be lord of it, and I'll serve thee.

STEPHANO How now shall this be compassed? Canst thou
   bring me to the party?

CALIBAN
Yea, yea, my lord. I'll yield him thee asleep,   60
Where thou mayst knock a nail into his head.

ARIEL Thou liest, thou canst not.

CALIBAN
What a pied ninny's this! Thou scurvy patch!
I do beseech thy greatness, give him blows,
And take his bottle from him. When that's gone,
He shall drink naught but brine, for I'll not show him
Where the quick freshes are.

STEPHANO Trinculo, run into no further danger. Interrupt
   the monster one word further, and by this hand, I'll
   turn my mercy out o'doors, and make a stockfish of   70
   thee.

TRINCULO Why, what did I? I did nothing. I'll go further
   off.

STEPHANO Didst thou not say he lied?

ARIEL Thou liest.

STEPHANO Do I so? Take thou that!
      He strikes Trinculo
   As you like this, give me the lie another time.

TRINCULO I did not give the lie. Out o'your wits, and
   hearing too? A pox o'your bottle! This can sack and
   drinking do. A murrain on your monster, and the devil   80
   take your fingers!

CALIBAN Ha, ha, ha!

STEPHANO Now forward with your tale. — Prithee stand
    farther off.

CALIBAN
    Beat him enough. After a little time
    I'll beat him too.

STEPHANO Stand farther. — Come, proceed.

CALIBAN
    Why, as I told thee, 'tis a custom with him
    I'th'afternoon to sleep. There thou mayst brain him,
90 Having first seized his books; or with a log
    Batter his skull, or paunch him with a stake,
    Or cut his weasand with thy knife. Remember
    First to possess his books, for without them
    He's but a sot as I am, nor hath not
    One spirit to command: they all do hate him
    As rootedly as I. Burn but his books.
    He has brave utensils, for so he calls them,
    Which, when he has a house, he'll deck withal.
    And that most deeply to consider is
100 The beauty of his daughter. He himself
    Calls her a nonpareil. I never saw a woman
    But only Sycorax, my dam, and she,
    But she as far surpasseth Sycorax
    As great'st does least.

STEPHANO   Is it so brave a lass?

CALIBAN
    Ay, lord. She will become thy bed, I warrant,
    And bring thee forth brave brood.

STEPHANO Monster, I will kill this man. His daughter and
    I will be king and queen — save our graces! — and
    Trinculo and thyself shall be viceroys. Dost thou like
110 the plot, Trinculo?

TRINCULO Excellent.

STEPHANO Give me thy hand. I am sorry I beat thee, but

(marginal annotation: Plotting)

(marginal annotation: No comparason with her beauty)

while thou liv'st keep a good tongue in thy head.

CALIBAN

<u>Within this half hour will he be asleep,</u>
<u>Wilt thou destroy him then?</u>

STEPHANO   Ay, on mine honour.

ARIEL This will I tell my master.

CALIBAN

Thou mak'st me merry. I am full of pleasure.
Let us be jocund. Will you troll the catch
You taught me but whilere?

STEPHANO At thy request, monster, I will do reason, any   120
reason. Come on, Trinculo, let us sing.

    Sings

        Flout 'em and scout 'em,
        And scout 'em and flout 'em.
          Thought is free.

CALIBAN That's not the tune.

    Ariel plays the tune on a tabor and pipe

STEPHANO What is this same?

TRINCULO This is the tune of our catch, played by the
picture of Nobody.

STEPHANO If thou beest a man, show thyself in thy like-
ness. If thou beest a devil, take't as thou list.   130

TRINCULO O, forgive me my sins!

STEPHANO He that dies pays all debts. I defy thee. Mercy
upon us!

CALIBAN Art thou afeard?

STEPHANO No, monster, not I.

CALIBAN

Be not afeard; the isle is full of noises,
Sounds, and sweet airs, that give delight and hurt not.
Sometimes a thousand twangling instruments
Will hum about mine ears; and sometime voices,
That if I then had waked after long sleep   140

love of music

Will make me sleep again; and then in dreaming,
The clouds methought would open, and show riches
Ready to drop upon me, that when I waked
I cried to dream again.

STEPHANO This will prove a brave kingdom to me, where
I shall have my music for nothing.

CALIBAN When Prospero is destroyed.

STEPHANO That shall be by and by. I remember the story.

Exit Ariel, playing music

TRINCULO The sound is going away. Let's follow it, and
150   after do our work.

STEPHANO Lead, monster, we'll follow. I would I could
see this taborer, he lays it on.

TRINCULO Wilt come? – I'll follow, Stephano.   *Exeunt*

III.3   *Enter Alonso, Sebastian, Antonio, Gonzalo, Adrian,*
       Francisco, and others

GONZALO
   By'r lakin, I can go no further, sir,
   My old bones aches. Here's a maze trod indeed,
   Through forthrights and meanders. By your patience,
   I needs must rest me.

ALONSO.   Old lord, I cannot blame thee,
   Who am myself attached with weariness
   To th'dulling of my spirits. Sit down and rest.
   Even here I will put off my hope, and keep it
   No longer for my flatterer. He is drowned
   Whom thus we stray to find, and the sea mocks
10   Our frustrate search on land. Well, let him go.

ANTONIO (*aside to Sebastian*)
   I am right glad that he's so out of hope.
   Do not for one repulse forgo the purpose
   That you resolved t'effect.

SEBASTIAN (*aside to Antonio*) The next advantage
    Will we take throughly.

ANTONIO   Let it be tonight;
    For now they are oppressed with travail, they
    Will not, nor cannot, use such vigilance
    As when they are fresh.

SEBASTIAN   I say tonight. No more.

    Solemn and strange music; and Prospero on the top,
    invisible. Enter several strange Shapes, bringing in a
    banquet, and dance about it with gentle actions of
    salutations; and inviting the King, etc., to eat, they
    depart

ALONSO

What harmony is this? My good friends, hark.

GONZALO

Marvellous sweet music!

ALONSO

Give us kind keepers, heavens! What were these?   20

SEBASTIAN

    A living drollery! Now I will believe
    That there are unicorns; that in Arabia
    There is one tree, the phoenix' throne, one phoenix
    At this hour reigning there.

ANTONIO   I'll believe both;
    And what does else want credit, come to me
    And I'll be sworn 'tis true. Travellers ne'er did lie,
    Though fools at home condemn 'em.

GONZALO   If in Naples
    I should report this now, would they believe me?
    If I should say I saw such islanders –
    For certes, these are people of the island –   30
    Who, though they are of monstrous shape, yet note
    Their manners are more gentle, kind, than of
    Our human generation you shall find

Many, nay almost any.

PROSPERO (*aside*)   Honest lord,
Thou hast said well, for some of you there present
Are worse than devils.

ALONSO   I cannot too much muse
Such shapes, such gesture, and such sound, expressing –
Although they want the use of tongue – a kind
Of excellent dumb discourse.

PROSPERO (*aside*)   Praise in departing.

FRANCISCO
40   They vanished strangely.

SEBASTIAN   No matter, since
They have left their viands behind, for we have stom-
     achs.
Will't please you taste of what is here?

ALONSO   Not I.

GONZALO
Faith, sir, you need not fear. When we were boys,
Who would believe that there were mountaineers
Dewlapped like bulls, whose throats had hanging at 'em
Wallets of flesh? Or that there were such men
Whose heads stood in their breasts? Which now we find
Each putter-out of five for one will bring us
Good warrant of.

ALONSO   I will stand to and feed,
50   Although my last – no matter, since I feel
The best is past. Brother, my lord the Duke,
Stand to and do as we.

     Thunder and lightning. Enter Ariel, like a harpy,
     claps his wings upon the table, and with a quaint
     device the banquet vanishes

ARIEL
You are three men of sin, whom destiny,
That hath to instrument this lower world

And what is in't, the never-surfeited sea
Hath caused to belch up you, and on this island,
Where man doth not inhabit – you 'mongst men
Being most unfit to live. I have made you mad;
And even with suchlike valour, men hang and drown
Their proper selves.

Alonso, Sebastian, and Antonio draw their swords
                You fools! I and my fellows   60
Are ministers of Fate. The elements
Of whom your swords are tempered may as well
Wound the loud winds, or with bemocked-at stabs
Kill the still-closing waters, as diminish
One dowl that's in my plume. My fellow ministers
Are like invulnerable. If you could hurt,
Your swords are now too massy for your strengths,
And will not be uplifted. But remember –
For that's my business to you – that you three
From Milan did supplant good Prospero,   70
Exposed unto the sea, which hath requit it,
Him and his innocent child; for which foul deed,
The powers, delaying, not forgetting, have
Incensed the seas and shores, yea, all the creatures
Against your peace. Thee of thy son, Alonso,
They have bereft; and do pronounce by me
Ling'ring perdition, worse than any death
Can be at once, shall step by step attend
You and your ways; whose wraths to guard you from –
Which here, in this most desolate isle, else falls   80
Upon your heads – is nothing but heart's sorrow
And a clear life ensuing.

He vanishes in thunder; then, to soft music, enter the
Shapes again, and dance with mocks and mows, and
carry out the table

PROSPERO
    Bravely the figure of this harpy hast thou
    Performed, my Ariel; a grace it had, devouring.
    Of my instruction hast thou nothing bated
    In what thou hadst to say; so, with good life
    And observation strange, my meaner ministers
    Their several kinds have done. My high charms work,
    And these, mine enemies, are all knit up
    In their distractions. They now are in my power;
    And in these fits I leave them, while I visit
    Young Ferdinand, whom they suppose is drowned,
    And his and mine loved darling.   *Exit*

GONZALO
    I'th'name of something holy, sir, why stand you
    In this strange stare?

ALONSO   O, it is monstrous, monstrous!
    Methought the billows spoke, and told me of it,
    The winds did sing it to me, and the thunder,
    That deep and dreadful organ-pipe, pronounced
    The name of Prosper. It did bass my trespass.
100   Therefore my son i'th'ooze is bedded, and
    I'll seek him deeper than e'er plummet sounded,
    And with him there lie mudded.   *Exit*

SEBASTIAN   But one fiend at a time,
    I'll fight their legions o'er!

ANTONIO   I'll be thy second.
                     Exeunt Antonio and Sebastian

GONZALO
    All three of them are desperate. Their great guilt,
    Like poison given to work a great time after,
    Now 'gins to bite the spirits. I do beseech you,
    That are of suppler joints, follow them swiftly,
    And hinder them from what this ecstasy

Nature v Nature.
Naturally about what your
taught.

May now provoke them to.

ADRIAN   Follow, I pray you.

Exeunt

*

Enter Prospero, Ferdinand, and Miranda   **IV.1**

PROSPERO (*to Ferdinand*)

If I have too austerely punished you,   *Made him want*
                                               to prove himself
Your compensation makes amends, for I   *worthy*
Have given you here a third of mine own life, *Miranda*
                                               is ⅓ of his
Or that for which I live; who once again   *life.*
I tender to thy hand. All thy vexations
Were but my trials of thy love, and thou
Hast strangely stood the test. Here, afore heaven,
I ratify this my rich gift. O Ferdinand,
Do not smile at me that I boast of her,
For thou shalt find she will outstrip all praise — *She's beyond* 10
And make it halt behind her.   *perfect.*

FERDINAND   I do believe it
Against an oracle.

PROSPERO

Then as my gift, and thine own acquisition
Worthily purchased, take my daughter. But
If thou dost break her virgin-knot before
All sanctimonious ceremonies may
With full and holy rite be ministered,
No sweet aspersion shall the heavens let fall
To make this contract grow; but barren hate,
Sour-eyed disdain and discord shall bestrew   20
The union of your bed with weeds so loathly
That you shall hate it both. Therefore take heed,

Knowlege will destroy her.

As Hymen's lamps shall light you.

FERDINAND   As I hope
For quiet days, fair issue, and long life,
With such love as 'tis now, the murkiest den,
The most opportune place, the strong'st suggestion
Our worser genius can, shall never melt
Mine honour into lust, to take away
The edge of that day's celebration,
When I shall think or Phoebus' steeds are foundered
Or night kept chained below.

PROSPERO   Fairly spoke.
Sit, then, and talk with her; she is thine own. –
What, Ariel! My industrious servant, Ariel!

   Enter Ariel

ARIEL
What would my potent master? Here I am.

PROSPERO
Thou and thy meaner fellows your last service
Did worthily perform, and I must use you
In such another trick. Go bring the rabble,
O'er whom I give thee power, here to this place.
Incite them to quick motion, for I must
Bestow upon the eyes of this young couple
Some vanity of mine art. It is my promise,
And they expect it from me.

ARIEL   Presently?

PROSPERO
Ay, with a twink.

ARIEL
Before you can say 'come' and 'go',
And breathe twice, and cry 'so, so',
Each one tripping on his toe
Will be here with mop and mow.
Do you love me, master? No?

PROSPERO
    Dearly, my delicate Ariel. Do not approach
    Till thou dost hear me call.

ARIEL   Well, I conceive.   *Exit* 50

PROSPERO (*to Ferdinand*)
    Look thou be true. Do not give dalliance
    Too much the rein. The strongest oaths are straw
    To th'fire i'th'blood. Be more abstemious,
    Or else good night your vow.

FERDINAND   I warrant you, sir,
    The white cold virgin snow upon my heart
    Abates the ardour of my liver.

PROSPERO   Well. –
    Now come, my Ariel. Bring a corollary,
    Rather than want a spirit. Appear, and pertly.
      Soft music
    No tongue! All eyes! Be silent.
      Enter Iris

IRIS
    Ceres, most bounteous lady, thy rich leas   60
    Of wheat, rye, barley, vetches, oats, and pease;
    Thy turfy mountains, where live nibbling sheep,
    And flat meads thatched with stover, them to keep;
    Thy banks with peonied and twillèd brims,
    Which spongy April at thy hest betrims,
    To make cold nymphs chaste crowns; and thy broom-
        groves,
    Whose shadow the dismissèd bachelor loves,
    Being lass-lorn; thy pole-clipped vineyard,
    And thy sea-marge, sterile and rocky-hard,
    Where thou thyself dost air – the queen o'th'sky,   70
    Whose watery arch and messenger am I,
    Bids thee leave these, and with her sovereign grace,
      Juno descends

Here on this grass-plot, in this very place
To come and sport. Her peacocks fly amain.
Approach, rich Ceres, her to entertain.
    Enter Ceres

CERES
Hail, many-coloured messenger, that ne'er
Dost disobey the wife of Jupiter;
Who, with thy saffron wings, upon my flowers
Diffusest honey-drops, refreshing showers,
80   And with each end of thy blue bow dost crown
My bosky acres and my unshrubbed down,
Rich scarf to my proud earth. Why hath thy queen
Summoned me hither to this short-grassed green?

IRIS
A contract of true love to celebrate,
And some donation freely to estate
On the blessed lovers.

CERES   Tell me, heavenly bow,
If Venus or her son, as thou dost know,
Do now attend the queen? Since they did plot
The means that dusky Dis my daughter got,
90   Her and her blind boy's scandalled company
I have forsworn.

IRIS   Of her society
Be not afraid. I met her deity
Cutting the clouds towards Paphos, and her son
Dove-drawn with her. Here thought they to have done
Some wanton charm upon this man and maid,
Whose vows are that no bed-right shall be paid
Till Hymen's torch be lighted: but in vain.
Mars's hot minion is returned again;
Her waspish-headed son has broke his arrows,
100   Swears he will shoot no more, but play with sparrows,
And be a boy right out.

CERES   Highest queen of state,
  Great Juno comes; I know her by her gait.
JUNO
  How does my bounteous sister? Go with me
  To bless this twain, that they may prosperous be,
  And honoured in their issue.
        They sing
JUNO
              Honour, riches, marriage-blessing,
              Long continuance and increasing,
              Hourly joys be still upon you,
              Juno sings her blessings on you.

CERES
              Earth's increase, foison plenty,   110
              Barns and garners never empty,
              Vines with clust'ring bunches growing,
              Plants with goodly burden bowing;
              Spring come to you at the farthest,
              In the very end of harvest.
              Scarcity and want shall shun you,
              Ceres' blessing so is on you.

FERDINAND
  This is a most majestic vision, and
  Harmonious charmingly. May I be bold
  To think these spirits?
PROSPERO   Spirits, which by mine art   120
  I have from their confines called to enact
  My present fancies.
FERDINAND   Let me live here ever!
  So rare a wondered father and a wife
  Makes this place paradise.
PROSPERO   Sweet now, silence.
  Juno and Ceres whisper seriously,
  There's something else to do. Hush, and be mute,

Or else our spell is marred.

Juno and Ceres whisper, and send Iris on employment

IRIS

You nymphs, called naiads, of the windring brooks,
With your sedged crowns and ever-harmless looks,
130 Leave your crisp channels, and on this green land
Answer your summons; Juno does command.
Come, temperate nymphs, and help to celebrate
A contract of true love. Be not too late.

Enter certain Nymphs

You sunburned sicklemen, of August weary,
Come hither from the furrow, and be merry,
Make holiday; your rye-straw hats put on,
And these fresh nymphs encounter every one
In country footing.

*Enter certain Reapers, properly habited. They join
with the Nymphs in a graceful dance, towards the end
whereof Prospero starts suddenly and speaks; after
which, to a strange, hollow, and confused noise, they
heavily vanish*

PROSPERO (*aside*)

I had forgot that foul conspiracy
140 Of the beast Caliban and his confederates
Against my life. The minute of their plot
Is almost come. – Well done! Avoid, no more!

FERDINAND

This is strange. Your father's in some passion
That works him strongly.

MIRANDA   Never till this day
Saw I him touched with anger so distempered.

PROSPERO

You do look, my son, in a moved sort,
As if you were dismayed. Be cheerful, sir.
Our revels now are ended. These our actors,

As I foretold you, were all spirits, and
Are melted into air, into thin air;   150
And, like the baseless fabric of this vision,
The cloud-capped towers, the gorgeous palaces,
The solemn temples, the great globe itself,
Yea, all which it inherit, shall dissolve,
And like this insubstantial pageant faded,
Leave not a rack behind. We are such stuff
As dreams are made on, and our little life
Is rounded with a sleep. Sir, I am vexed.
Bear with my weakness; my old brain is troubled.
Be not disturbed with my infirmity.   160
If you be pleased, retire into my cell,
And there repose. A turn or two I'll walk
To still my beating mind.

FERDINAND *and* MIRANDA We wish your peace.
                    Exeunt Ferdinand and Miranda

PROSPERO
Come with a thought. I thank thee, Ariel. Come!
    Enter Ariel

ARIEL
Thy thoughts I cleave to. What's thy pleasure?

PROSPERO   Spirit,
We must prepare to meet with Caliban.

ARIEL
Ay, my commander. When I presented Ceres
I thought to have told thee of it, but I feared
Lest I might anger thee.

PROSPERO
Say again, where didst thou leave these varlets?   170

ARIEL
I told you, sir, they were red-hot with drinking,
So full of valour that they smote the air

[handwritten margin notes: "Trusts them not to do anything even when alone in bed together."; "Evil person"; "Tool of change."]

Ariel has dragged them on a wild goose chase.

For breathing in their faces, beat the ground
For kissing of their feet; yet always bending
Towards their project. Then I beat my tabor,
At which, like unbacked colts, they pricked their ears,
Advanced their eyelids, lifted up their noses
As they smelt music. So I charmed their ears
That calf-like they my lowing followed, through
180   Toothed briars, sharp furzes, pricking gorse, and thorns,
Which entered their frail shins. At last I left them
I'th'filthy-mantled pool beyond your cell,
There dancing up to th'chins, that the foul lake
O'erstunk their feet.

PROSPERO   This was well done, my bird.
Thy shape invisible retain thou still.
The trumpery in my house, go bring it hither,
For stale to catch these thieves.

ARIEL   I go, I go!   *Exit*

PROSPERO
A devil, a born devil, on whose nature
Nurture can never stick; on whom my pains,
190   Humanely taken, all, all lost, quite lost;
And, as with age his body uglier grows,
So his mind cankers. I will plague them all,
Even to roaring.
    Enter Ariel, loaden with glistering apparel, etc.
            Come, hang them on this line.
    Enter Caliban, Stephano, and Trinculo, all wet

CALIBAN Pray you tread softly, that the blind mole may
not hear a footfall. We now are near his cell.

STEPHANO Monster, your fairy, which you say is a
harmless fairy, has done little better than played the
jack with us.

TRINCULO Monster, I do smell all horse-piss, at which my
200   nose is in great indignation.

STEPHANO So is mine. Do you hear, monster? If I should
  take a displeasure against you, look you —

TRINCULO Thou wert but a lost monster.

CALIBAN

  Good my lord, give me thy favour still.
  Be patient, for the prize I'll bring thee to
  Shall hoodwink this mischance. Therefore speak softly;
  All's hushed as midnight yet.

TRINCULO Ay, but to lose our bottles in the pool —

STEPHANO There is not only disgrace and dishonour in
  that, monster, but an infinite loss.   210

TRINCULO That's more to me than my wetting. Yet this
  is your harmless fairy, monster.

STEPHANO I will fetch off my bottle, though I be o'er ears
  for my labour.

CALIBAN

  Prithee, my king, be quiet. Seest thou here,
  This is the mouth o'th'cell. No noise, and enter.
  Do that good mischief which may make this island
  Thine own forever, and I, thy Caliban,
  For aye thy foot-licker.

STEPHANO Give me thy hand. I do begin to have bloody   220
  thoughts.

TRINCULO O King Stephano! O peer! O worthy Stephano,
  look what a wardrobe here is for thee!

CALIBAN

  Let it alone, thou fool, it is but trash.

TRINCULO O ho, monster! We know what belongs to a
  frippery. O King Stephano!

STEPHANO Put off that gown, Trinculo. By this hand, I'll
  have that gown!

TRINCULO Thy grace shall have it.

CALIBAN

  The dropsy drown this fool! What do you mean   230

To dote thus on such luggage? Let't alone
And do the murder first. If he awake,
From toe to crown he'll fill our skins with pinches,
Make us strange stuff.

STEPHANO Be you quiet, monster. Mistress line, is not this
my jerkin? Now is the jerkin under the line. Now, jerkin,
you are like to lose your hair, and prove a bald jerkin.

TRINCULO Do, do! We steal by line and level, an't like
your grace.

240 STEPHANO I thank thee for that jest; here's a garment
for't. Wit shall not go unrewarded while I am king of
this country. 'Steal by line and level' is an excellent pass
of pate. There's another garment for't.

TRINCULO Monster, come put some lime upon your
fingers, and away with the rest.

CALIBAN
I will have none on't. We shall lose our time,
And all be turned to barnacles, or to apes
With foreheads villainous low.

STEPHANO Monster, lay to your fingers. Help to bear this
250 away where my hogshead of wine is, or I'll turn you
out of my kingdom. Go to, carry this.

TRINCULO And this.

STEPHANO Ay, and this.

*A noise of hunters heard. Enter divers Spirits in shape
of dogs and hounds, hunting them about, Prospero
and Ariel setting them on*

PROSPERO Hey, Mountain, hey!

ARIEL Silver! There it goes, Silver!

PROSPERO Fury, Fury! There, Tyrant, there! Hark, hark!
The Spirits drive out Caliban, Stephano, and Trinculo
Go, charge my goblins that they grind their joints
With dry convulsions, shorten up their sinews
With agèd cramps, and more pinch-spotted make them

Than pard or cat-o'-mountain.

ARIEL   Hark, they roar!   260

PROSPERO

Let them be hunted soundly. At this hour
Lies at my mercy all mine enemies.
Shortly shall all my labours end, and thou
Shalt have the air at freedom. For a little
Follow, and do me service.   *Exeunt*

*

Enter Prospero, in his magic robes, and Ariel   V.I

PROSPERO

Now does my project gather to a head.
My charms crack not, my spirits obey, and time
Goes upright with his carriage. How's the day?

ARIEL

On the sixth hour; at which time, my lord,
You said our work should cease.

PROSPERO   I did say so,
When first I raised the tempest. Say, my spirit,
How fares the King and's followers?

ARIEL   Confined together
In the same fashion as you gave in charge,
Just as you left them; all prisoners, sir,
In the line-grove which weather-fends your cell.   10
They cannot budge till your release. The King,
His brother, and yours, abide all three distracted,
And the remainder mourning over them,
Brimful of sorrow and dismay; but chiefly
Him that you termed, sir, the good old lord Gonzalo.
His tears run down his beard like winter's drops
From eaves of reeds. Your charm so strongly works 'em

That, if you now beheld them, your affections
Would become tender.

PROSPERO   Dost thou think so, spirit?

ARIEL

20   Mine would, sir, were I human.

PROSPERO   And mine shall.
Hast thou, which art but air, a touch, a feeling
Of their afflictions, and shall not myself,
One of their kind, that relish all as sharply
Passion as they, be kindlier moved than thou art?
Though with their high wrongs I am struck to th'quick,
Yet with my nobler reason 'gainst my fury
Do I take part. The rarer action is
In virtue than in vengeance. They being penitent,
The sole drift of my purpose doth extend

30   Not a frown further. Go, release them, Ariel.
My charms I'll break, their senses I'll restore,
And they shall be themselves.

ARIEL   I'll fetch them, sir. *Exit*

PROSPERO (*tracing a circle*)
Ye elves of hills, brooks, standing lakes, and groves,
And ye that on the sands with printless foot
Do chase the ebbing Neptune, and do fly him
When he comes back; you demi-puppets, that
By moonshine do the green sour ringlets make,
Whereof the ewe not bites; and you, whose pastime
Is to make midnight mushrooms, that rejoice

40   To hear the solemn curfew; by whose aid –
Weak masters though ye be – I have bedimmed
The noontide sun, called forth the mutinous winds,
And 'twixt the green sea and the azured vault
Set roaring war; to the dread rattling thunder
Have I given fire, and rifted Jove's stout oak
With his own bolt; the strong-based promontory

sared people

Have I made shake, and by the spurs plucked up
The pine and cedar; graves at my command
Have waked their sleepers, oped and let 'em forth
By my so potent art. But this rough magic   50
I here abjure; and when I have required
Some heavenly music – which even now I do –
To work mine end upon their senses that
This airy charm is for, I'll break my staff,   *once he's*
Bury it certain fathoms in the earth,   *achieved every-*
And deeper than did ever plummet sound   *thing he will*
I'll drown my book.   *get rid of his*

    Solemn music. Here enters Ariel before; then Alonso *magical*
    with a frantic gesture, attended by Gonzalo;   *stuff.*
    Sebastian and Antonio in like manner, attended by
    Adrian and Francisco. They all enter the circle which
    Prospero had made, and there stand charmed; which   *Judgment*
    Prospero observing, speaks   *Apocalyptic.*

A solemn air, and the best comforter
To an unsettled fancy, cure thy brains,
Now useless, boiled within thy skull. There stand,   60
For you are spell-stopped.
Holy Gonzalo, honourable man,
Mine eyes, ev'n sociable to the show of thine,
Fall fellowly drops. The charm dissolves apace,
And as the morning steals upon the night,
Melting the darkness, so their rising senses
Begin to chase the ignorant fumes that mantle
Their clearer reason. O good Gonzalo,
My true preserver and a loyal sir
To him thou follow'st, I will pay thy graces   70
Home both in word and deed. Most cruelly
Didst thou, Alonso, use me and my daughter.
Thy brother was a furtherer in the act:
Thou art pinched for't now, Sebastian. Flesh and blood,

You, brother mine, that entertained ambition,
Expelled remorse and nature, who with Sebastian —
Whose inward pinches therefore are most strong —
Would here have killed your king: I do forgive thee,
Unnatural though thou art. Their understanding
80   Begins to swell, and the approaching tide
Will shortly fill the reasonable shore
That now lies foul and muddy. Not one of them
That yet looks on me, or would know me. Ariel,
Fetch me the hat and rapier in my cell.
I will discase me, and myself present
As I was sometime Milan. Quickly, spirit,
Thou shalt ere long be free.
       Ariel sings, and helps to attire him

ARIEL
       Where the bee sucks, there suck I,
       In a cowslip's bell I lie;
90   There I couch when owls do cry.
       On the bat's back I do fly
              After summer merrily.
       Merrily, merrily shall I live now,
       Under the blossom that hangs on the bough.

PROSPERO
       Why, that's my dainty Ariel! I shall miss
Thee, but yet thou shalt have freedom. So, so, so.
To the King's ship, invisible as thou art;
There shalt thou find the mariners asleep
Under the hatches. The Master and the Boatswain
100   Being awake, enforce them to this place,
And presently, I prithee.

ARIEL
       I drink the air before me, and return
Or ere your pulse twice beat.   *Exit*

GONZALO

  All torment, trouble, wonder, and amazement   *Confussed.*
  Inhabits here. Some heavenly power guide us
  Out of this fearful country!

PROSPERO   Behold, sir King,
  The wrongèd Duke of Milan, Prospero.
  For more assurance that a living prince
  Does now speak to thee, I embrace thy body,
  And to thee and thy company I bid   110
  A hearty welcome.

ALONSO   Whe'er thou beest he or no,
  Or some enchanted trifle to abuse me,
  As late I have been, I not know. Thy pulse
  Beats as of flesh and blood, and since I saw thee,
  Th'affliction of my mind amends, with which
  I fear a madness held me. This must crave –
  An if this be at all – a most strange story.
  Thy dukedom I resign, and do entreat
  Thou pardon me my wrongs. But how should Prospero
  Be living, and be here?

PROSPERO (*to Gonzalo*)   First, noble friend,   120
  Let me embrace thine age, whose honour cannot
  Be measured or confined.

GONZALO   Whether this be
  Or be not, I'll not swear.

PROSPERO   You do yet taste
  Some subtleties o'th'isle, that will not let you
  Believe things certain. Welcome, my friends all!
  (*Aside to Sebastian and Antonio*)
  But you, my brace of lords, were I so minded
  I here could pluck his highness' frown upon you
  And justify you traitors. At this time
  I will tell no tales.

SEBASTIAN   The devil speaks in him!

PROSPERO   No.

130   For you, most wicked sir, whom to call brother
        Would even infect my mouth, I do forgive
        Thy rankest fault – all of them – and require
        My dukedom of thee, which perforce I know
        Thou must restore.

ALONSO   If thou beest Prospero,
        Give us particulars of thy preservation;
        How thou hast met us here, whom three hours since
        Were wrecked upon this shore, where I have lost –
        How sharp the point of this remembrance is –
        My dear son Ferdinand.

PROSPERO   I am woe for't, sir.

ALONSO

140   Irreparable is the loss, and patience
        Says it is past her cure.

PROSPERO   I rather think
        You have not sought her help, of whose soft grace
        For the like loss I have her sovereign aid,
        And rest myself content.

ALONSO   You the like loss?

PROSPERO
        As great to me, as late; and supportable
        To make the dear loss, have I means much weaker
        Than you may call to comfort you, for I
        Have lost my daughter.

ALONSO   A daughter?
        O heavens, that they were living both in Naples

150   The king and queen there! That they were, I wish
        Myself were mudded in that oozy bed
        Where my son lies. When did you lose your daughter?

PROSPERO
        In this last tempest. I perceive these lords
        At this encounter do so much admire

That they devour their reason, and scarce think
Their eyes do offices of truth, their words
Are natural breath. But howsoe'er you have
Been jostled from your senses, know for certain
That I am Prospero, and that very duke
Which was thrust forth of Milan, who most strangely   160
Upon this shore, where you were wrecked, was landed
To be the lord on't. No more yet of this,
For 'tis a chronicle of day by day,
Not a relation for a breakfast, nor
Befitting this first meeting. Welcome, sir.
This cell's my court; here have I few attendants,
And subjects none abroad. Pray you, look in.
My dukedom since you have given me again,
I will requite you with as good a thing,
At least bring forth a wonder to content ye   170
As much as me my dukedom.

Here Prospero discovers Ferdinand and Miranda,
playing at <u>chess</u> strategic game.

MIRANDA
Sweet lord, you play me false.
FERDINAND   No, my dearest love,
I would not for the world.
MIRANDA
Yes, for a score of kingdoms you should wrangle,
And I would call it fair play.
ALONSO   If this prove
A vision of the island, one dear son
Shall I twice lose.
SEBASTIAN   A most high miracle!
FERDINAND (*seeing Alonso*)
Though the seas threaten, they are merciful.
I have cursed them without cause.
He kneels before Alonso

ALONSO   Now all the blessings
Of a glad father compass thee about!
Arise, and say how thou cam'st here.

MIRANDA   O wonder!
How many goodly creatures are there here!
How beauteous mankind is! O brave new world,
That has such people in't!

PROSPERO   'Tis new to thee.

ALONSO
What is this maid with whom thou wast at play?
Your eld'st acquaintance cannot be three hours.
Is she the goddess that hath severed us,
And brought us thus together?

FERDINAND   Sir, she is mortal,
But by immortal providence, she's mine.
I chose her when I could not ask my father
For his advice, nor thought I had one. She
Is daughter to this famous Duke of Milan,
Of whom so often I have heard renown,
But never saw before; of whom I have
Received a second life, and second father
This lady makes him to me.

ALONSO   I am hers.
But O, how oddly will it sound that I
Must ask my child forgiveness?

PROSPERO   There, sir, stop.
Let us not burden our remembrances with
A heaviness that's gone.

GONZALO   I have inly wept,
Or should have spoke ere this. Look down, you gods,
And on this couple drop a blessèd crown!
For it is you that have chalked forth the way
Which brought us hither.

ALONSO   I say amen, Gonzalo.

GONZALO

    Was Milan thrust from Milan, that his issue
    Should become kings of Naples? O, rejoice
    Beyond a common joy, and set it down
    With gold on lasting pillars: in one voyage
    Did Claribel her husband find at Tunis,
    And Ferdinand her brother found a wife   210
    Where he himself was lost; Prospero, his dukedom
    In a poor isle; and all of us ourselves,
    When no man was his own.

ALONSO (*to Ferdinand and Miranda*) Give me your hands.
    Let grief and sorrow still embrace his heart
    That doth not wish you joy.

GONZALO   Be it so, amen.

    Enter Ariel, with the Master and Boatswain
      amazedly following

    O look, sir, look sir, here is more of us!
    I prophesied, if a gallows were on land,
    This fellow could not drown. Now, blasphemy,
    That swear'st grace o'erboard, not an oath on shore?
    Hast thou no mouth by land? What is the news?   220

BOATSWAIN

    The best news is that we have safely found
    Our King and company; the next, our ship,
    Which but three glasses since we gave out split,
    Is tight and yare and bravely rigged as when
    We first put out to sea.

ARIEL (*aside to Prospero*) Sir, all this service
    Have I done since I went.

PROSPERO (*aside to Ariel*) My tricksy spirit!

ALONSO

    These are not natural events; they strengthen
    From strange to stranger. Say, how came you hither?

BOATSWAIN

    If I did think, sir, I were well awake,
230   I'd strive to tell you. We were dead of sleep,
    And – how we know not – all clapped under hatches,
    Where, but even now, with strange and several noises
    Of roaring, shrieking, howling, jingling chains,
    And more diversity of sounds, all horrible,
    We were awaked, straightway at liberty;
    Where we, in all our trim, freshly beheld
    Our royal, good and gallant ship, our Master
    Cap'ring to eye her. On a trice, so please you,
    Even in a dream, were we divided from them,
240   And were brought moping hither.

ARIEL (*aside to Prospero*)   Was't well done?

PROSPERO (*aside to Ariel*)

    Bravely, my diligence. Thou shalt be free.

ALONSO

    This is as strange a maze as e'er men trod,
    And there is in this business more than nature
    Was ever conduct of. Some oracle
    Must rectify our knowledge.

PROSPERO   Sir, my liege,

    Do not infest your mind with beating on
    The strangeness of this business. At picked leisure,
    Which shall be shortly, single I'll resolve you,
    Which to you shall seem probable, of every
250   These happened accidents. Till when, be cheerful,
    And think of each thing well. (*Aside to Ariel*) Come
        hither, spirit.
    Set Caliban and his companions free.
    Untie the spell.   *Exit Ariel*
            How fares my gracious sir?
    There are yet missing of your company
    Some few odd lads, that you remember not.

Enter Ariel, driving in Caliban, Stephano, and
Trinculo in their stolen apparel

STEPHANO Every man shift for all the rest, and let no man
take care for himself, for all is but fortune. Coragio,
bully-monster, coragio!

TRINCULO If these be true spies which I wear in my head,
here's a goodly sight!   260

CALIBAN
O Setebos, these be brave spirits indeed!
How fine my master is! I am afraid
He will chastise me.

SEBASTIAN   Ha, ha!
What things are these, my lord Antonio?
Will money buy 'em?

ANTONIO   Very like. One of them
Is a plain fish, and no doubt marketable.

PROSPERO
Mark but the badges of these men, my lords,
Then say if they be true. This misshapen knave,
His mother was a witch, and one so strong
That could control the moon, make flows and ebbs,   270
And deal in her command without her power.
These three have robbed me, and this demi-devil —
For he's a bastard one — had plotted with them
To take my life. Two of these fellows you
Must know and own; this thing of darkness I
Acknowledge mine.

CALIBAN   I shall be pinched to death.

ALONSO
Is not this Stephano, my drunken butler?

SEBASTIAN
He is drunk now. Where had he wine?

ALONSO
And Trinculo is reeling ripe. Where should they

280   Find this grand liquor that hath gilded 'em?
        How cam'st thou in this pickle?

TRINCULO I have been in such a pickle since I saw you
        last, that I fear me will never out of my bones. I shall
        not fear fly-blowing.

SEBASTIAN Why, how now, Stephano?

STEPHANO O touch me not! I am not Stephano, but a
        cramp.

PROSPERO You'd be king o'the isle, sirrah?

STEPHANO I should have been a sore one, then.

ALONSO

290   This is a strange thing as e'er I looked on.

PROSPERO
        He is as disproportioned in his manners
        As in his shape. – Go, sirrah, to my cell.
        Take with you your companions. As you look
        To have my pardon, trim it handsomely.

CALIBAN
        Ay, that I will; and I'll be wise hereafter,
        And seek for grace. What a thrice double ass
        Was I to take this drunkard for a god,
        And worship this dull fool!

PROSPERO   Go to, away.

ALONSO
        Hence, and bestow your luggage where you found it.

SEBASTIAN

300   Or stole it, rather.

                        Exeunt Caliban, Stephano, and Trinculo

PROSPERO
        Sir, I invite your highness and your train
        To my poor cell, where you shall take your rest
        For this one night, which, part of it, I'll waste
        With such discourse as I not doubt shall make it
        Go quick away – the story of my life,

And the particular accidents gone by
Since I came to this isle. And in the morn
I'll bring you to your ship, and so to Naples,
Where I have hope to see the nuptial
Of these our dear-belov'd solemnizèd;   310
And thence retire me to my Milan, where
Every third thought shall be my grave.

ALONSO   I long
To hear the story of your life, which must
Take the ear strangely.

PROSPERO   I'll deliver all,
And promise you calm seas, auspicious gales,
And sail so expeditious, that shall catch
Your royal fleet far off. – My Ariel, chick,
That is thy charge. Then to the elements
Be free, and fare thou well. – Please you draw near.

Exeunt all but Prospero

[handwritten margin note: No longer needs his magic so decides to give it away.]

[handwritten notes at bottom:]
Changes in relationship's.

Chain of being
Alcohol

Epilogue

Spoken by Prospero
Now my charms are all o'erthrown,
And what strength I have's mine own,
Which is most faint. Now 'tis true
I must be here confined by you,
Or sent to Naples. Let me not,
Since I have my dukedom got
And pardoned the deceiver, dwell
In this bare island by your spell;
But release me from my bands
10 With the help of your good hands.
Gentle breath of yours my sails
Must fill, or else my project fails,
Which was to please. Now I want
Spirits to enforce, art to enchant,
And my ending is despair
Unless I be relieved by prayer,
Which pierces so, that it assaults
Mercy itself, and frees all faults.
As you from crimes would pardoned be,
20 Let your indulgence set me free.   *Exit*

An Account of the Text

The Tempest was first printed in the 1623 Folio of Shakespeare's collected plays (abbreviated as F in the following tables). All subsequent editions derive from this source. The play stands first in the volume and had been prepared with great care. There are only a few passages that present editors with difficulties or require corrections. The most vexing of these are two unsolvable cruxes, *scamels* at II.2.172 and *wife* at IV.1.123.

Modern scholarship has demonstrated that copy for the printer was written out by Ralph Crane, a scrivener who was employed by Shakespeare's company, the King's Men, on a number of projects. He probably worked either from the company's own prompt book of the play or from a text that derived in some more direct way from Shakespeare's working papers.

Crane was an expert copyist, though he was inclined to introduce presentational polishing or 'improvements' of his own into the texts that he copied. The stage directions (see Collation 2) are unusually full and descriptive, and some may have been added by him, perhaps on the basis of performances he had seen. He probably compiled the detailed list of characters and devised the descriptive glosses that it includes – hence *savage and deformed slave* is likely to be Crane's rather than Shakespeare's description of Caliban. There are frequent ambiguities in the arrangement of the verse when lines are split between two or more speakers, and occasional confusions between verse and prose, which suggest that Crane wrote prose passages in short lines which the printers sometimes mistook for verse. This is a particular problem in Caliban's speeches, since his language is so frequently pitched on the borderline between the two modes (see Collation 3). Sometimes the layout of the songs is confusing, as Crane left it unclear which parts were refrains sung by groups of singers. Editors adjust these as best they can, but there are considerable differences of opinion about how the first song, 'Come unto these yellow sands', should be presented. The Folio's punctuation presents another difficulty, for it is very heavy and occasionally eccentric, as is usual in texts associated with Crane. Modern editions invariably standardize Crane's idiosyncratic style, substituting a lighter punctuation more in line with current norms. These changes are frequent and are not listed in the collation tables below, unless they alter the meaning of a passage.

In the Folio the play is neatly divided into acts and scenes, each being prefaced with a standard form *Actus Primus, Scena Prima*, etc. These headings are likely to have been added by Crane, though the five-act division must have been intended by Shakespeare, for it corresponds to the custom at the King's Men's indoor playhouse, the Blackfriars, of having four breaks during a performance, for the sake of trimming the candles. The exit of Prospero and Ariel at the end of Act IV and their immediate re-entry at the beginning of Act V shows that a break in performance must have been originally anticipated at this point.

Like most other modern editions, this text modernizes the Folio's spellings where no substantive change of meaning is involved in replacing the old spelling with its modern equivalent, or where the old spelling simply preserves a lost pronunciation. So, for example, we read *savage* rather than *salvage*, *furze* for *firrs*, *Algiers* for *Argier*, *Bermudas* for *Bermoothes*, *gorse* for *gosse*, *bowsprit* for *bore-spritt*, *debauched* for *deboshed*, *more* for *mo*, *vetches* for *fetches* and *mushrooms* for *mushrumps*.

COLLATIONS

1 Emendations

Alterations to F of any consequence are listed below, with F's reading on the right of the square bracket and any explanatory comments in italics immediately afterwards.

The Characters in the Play

The Characters in the Play] Names of the Actors
(*this list is placed at the end of the text in* F)
Spirits in the masque] Spirits
Other spirits, courtiers] *not in* F

I.1

   8 *Ferdinand*] Ferdinando
  59 VOICES OFFSTAGE] *not in* F

I.2

  112 wi'th'] with
  165 steaded] steeded
  173 princes] Princesse
  194 bade] bad
  242 thou] y^u
  248 made no] made thee no
  282 she] he
  301 like to] like
  380 the burden bear] *beare the burthen*
382–3 The watch-dogs bark. | Bow-wow, bow-wow] *bowgh
     wawgh: the watch-Dogges barke,* | *bowgh wawgh* (*addi-
     tionally, in* F *the stage direction is placed before 381*)
403–4 *lines reversed in* F
  415 thou] y^u

II.1

  38–9 *speech headings reversed in* F
   65 gloss] glosses
  202 consent;] consent
  230 throes] throwes

II.2

  182 trencher] trenchering

III.1

   2 sets] set
  15 busy, least] busie lest,
  47 peerless] peetlesse
  93 withal] with all

III.2

  122 scout] *cout*

III.3

   3 forthrights] fourth rights

    17 *Prospero*] *Prosper*
    29 islanders] Islands
    65 plume] plumbe
    82 *carry*] *carrying*
    99 bass] base

IV.I

     9 of her] her of
    13 gift] guest
    52 rein] raigne
    74 Her] here
   106 marriage-blessing] *marriage, blessing*
   110 CERES] *not in* F
   123 wife] wise (*in some copies; see Commentary note*)
   193 them on] on them
   231 Let't] let's

V.I

    16 run] runs
    60 boiled] boile
    72 Didst] Did
    75 entertained] entertaine
    76 who] whom
    82 lies] ly
   124 not] nor
   248 shortly, single] shortly single
   258 coragio] *Corasio*

2 Stage Directions

F's stage directions for *The Tempest* are unusually elaborate. In
most early modern texts based on theatrical manuscripts, the directions tend to be functional and terse, but in *The Tempest* they are
written in a literary style more suited to the needs of readers. For
example, where a dramatist writing a script for performance might
simply ask for 'Thunder and lightning', *The Tempest* has *A tempestuous noise of thunder and lightning heard*; instead of 'spirits' it has
the impractically vague phrase *several strange shapes*; and it once
replaces the theatrical term 'exeunt' with the more literary *they
depart*. Probably this language was supplied by the copyist,
Ralph Crane, or was worked up by him from Shakespeare's briefer

notations. For a full discussion, see the essay by John Jowett, 'New created creatures: Ralph Crane and the stage directions in *The Tempest*', *Shakespeare Survey 36* (1983), pp. 107–20.

In the present edition all asides and indications of the person to whom a speech is addressed are additions to the original text. Other changes are listed below, with F's reading to the right of the square bracket.

I.1

    33 *Exeunt courtiers*] *Exit.*

35, 37 *A cry within. Enter Sebastian, Antonio, and Gonzalo*] *printed together in F after* A plague

    61 *Exeunt Antonio and Sebastian*] *Exit.*

I.2

    24 *Miranda helps Prospero remove his gown*] *not in* F

  186 *Miranda sleeps*] *not in* F

  304 *Exit Ariel*] *Exit.*

  318 *(He whispers.)*] *not in* F

  466 *He draws his sword*] *He draws*

II.1

  188 *All sleep, except Alonso, Sebastian, and Antonio*] *not in* F

  196 *Alonso sleeps. Exit Ariel*] *not in* F

  296 *with music*] *with music and song*

  307 *(waking)*] *not in* F
           He shakes Alonso. The others awake] *not in* F

II.2

    17 *He lies down and covers himself with a cloak*] *not in* F

    24 *He sees Caliban.*] *not in* F

    36 *Thunder*] *not in* F

    41 *Trinculo hides under the cloak. Enter Stephano, singing, with a bottle*] *Enter Stephano singing.*

    45 *He drinks, then sings*] *Drinkes.* | *Sings.*

    55 *He drinks*] *drinks.*

85–6 *He gives Caliban wine, Caliban spits it out*] *not in* F

    94 *Caliban drinks.*] *not in* F

  105 *He pulls Trinculo out.*] *not in* F

  130 *Trinculo drinks.*] *not in* F

142–3 *Caliban drinks.*] *not in* F

III.1

  15 *Enter Miranda, and Prospero following at a distance*]
       Enter Miranda and Prospero.
  86 *(kneels)*] *not in* F
  91 *Exeunt Ferdinand and Miranda, in different directions*]
       Exeunt.

III.2

  76 *He strikes Trinculo*] *not in* F
 148 *Exit Ariel, playing music*] *not in* F

III.3

   0 *and others*] *&c.*
  17 *stage direction placed before* I say tonight
  60 *Alonso, Sebastian, and Antonio draw their swords*] *not
       in* F
  93 *Exit*] *not in* F
 103 *Exeunt Antonio and Sebastian*] *Exeunt.*
 109 *Exeunt*] *Exeunt omnes.*

IV.1

 163 *Exeunt Ferdinand and Miranda*] *Exit.*
 193 *Enter Ariel, loaden with glistering apparel, etc.*] *at end
       of line in* F
 256 *The Spirits drive out Caliban, Stephano, and Trinculo*]
       not in F

V.1

  33 *(tracing a circle)*] *not in* F
 178 *(seeing Alonso)*] *not in* F
 179 *He kneels before Alonso*] *not in* F
 253 *Exit Ariel*] *not in* F
 300 *Exeunt Caliban, Stephano, and Trinculo*] *not in* F
 319 *Exeunt all but Prospero*] *Exeunt omnes.*

3 Lineation

The lineation of F is a recurrent problem. There are several passages where the folio prints as verse speeches which appear to be prose, or prose as verse, and the arrangement of the verse is complicated by the high proportion of short lines or lines shared between two speakers. The adjustments to the lineation made in this edition are listed below, with F's readings to the right of the square bracket.

I.I

    54–6 *prose in* F

I.2

  309–10 'Tis ... look on] *one line in* F
    361–2 rock, | Who hadst deserved] Rocke, who hadst |
        Deseru'd

II.I

      18 entertained that's] entertaind, | That's
      30 wager, first] wager, | First
      55 looks! How] lookes? | How
  80–81 too? Good] too? | Good
  190–91 thoughts. I find | They] thoughts, | I finde they
  193–4 doth, | It] doth, it
  194–6 lord, | Will guard your person while you take your
      rest, | And watch] Lord, will guard your person, |
      While you take your rest, and watch
  243–4 Then ... Naples] *one line in* F

II.2

    42–3 I shall ... ashore] *one line in* F
      44 man's funeral] mans | Funerall
      55 too, but] too: | But
      57 matter? Have we devils here? Do] matter? | Haue
      we diuels here? | Doe
      88 voice. It should be – but] voyce: | It should be, | But
    119 'scape? How] scape? | How
    120 hither? Swear] hither? | Sweare
    130 book. Though] Booke. | Though
    134 hid. How] hid: | How
  145–6 monster! The Man i'th'Moon? A most poor credu-
      lous monster! – Well] Monster: | The Man
      ith'Moone? | A most poore creadulous monster: |
      Well
    158 drink. An] drinke. | An
  160–61 *prose in* F
  163–4 *prose in* F
  167–72 *prose in* F

III.2

    39 it. I] it, | I
    41–3 tyrant, a sorcerer, that by his cunning hath cheated

me of the island] Tirant, | A Sorcerer, that by his
cunning hath cheated me | Of the island
58 compassed? Canst] compast? | Canst
68 danger. Interrupt] danger: | Interrupt
72 nothing. I'll] nothing: | Ile
79–80 too? A pox o'your bottle! This can sack and drinking
do. A] too? | A pox o'your bottle, this can Sacke and
drinking doo: | A
109 viceroys. Dost] Vice-royes: | Dost
112 thee, but] thee: | But
120 reason, any] reason, | Any
132 thee. Mercy] thee; | Mercy
145 me, where] me, | Where
148 by. I] by: | I
149 away. Let's] away. | Lets
151–2 Lead, monster, we'll follow. I would I could see this
taborer, he lays it on] Leade Monster, | Wee'l
follow: I would I could see this Taborer, | He layes
it on

III.3
13–14 The ... throughly] *one line in* F
IV.1
165–6 Spirit | We ... Caliban] *one line in* F
197 fairy, has] Fairy, | Has
199 which my] which | My
201–2 should take] should | Take
211 wetting. Yet] wetting: | Yet
213 bottle, though] bottle, | Though
220 hand. I] hand, | I
222–3 Stephano, look] Stephano, | Looke
V.1
220 land? What] land? | What
256–7 let no man take care for himself, for all is but] let |
No man take care for himselfe: for all is | But
278 now. Where] now; | Where
283 last, that I fear me will never out of my bones. I]
last, | That I feare me will neuer out of my bones: | I

The Music

Contemporary music survives for two of *The Tempest*'s songs, 'Full fathom five' and 'Where the bee sucks'. These cannot be said for certain to be the settings used in the theatre, but it seems highly likely. The composer was Robert Johnson (d. 1633), who was one of the royal lutenists. He seems to have worked closely with the King's Men, for he made settings of songs for other plays in the company's repertoire by Ben Jonson, John Webster and John Fletcher, and he probably composed the music for 'Hark, hark, the lark' in *Cymbeline* and the song 'Come away, Hecate' inserted into *Macbeth*. His *Tempest* settings appear as solo songs in several manuscripts dating from the mid seventeenth century, and were printed in a modified form, with additional vocal parts for domestic performance, in a collection compiled by John Wilson, *Cheerful Ayres or Ballads* (1660). They have been edited by Ian Spink in *English Lute Songs*, second series 17 (1961; revised 1974).

There are recordings of both on *English Lute Songs*, performed by Robin Blaze and Elizabeth Kenny (Hyperion CDA 67126); on *Hark! Hark! The Lark!*, performed by Joseph Cornwell and the Parley of Instruments (Hyperion CDA 66836); on *Shakespeare's Lutenist*, performed by Emma Kirkby, David Thomas and Anthony Rooley (Virgin VC7593212); and on *Shakespeare Songs*, performed by Desmond Dupré and the Deller Consort (Deutsche Harmonia Mundi, 5472776922).

A dance tune named 'The Tempest' is included in a British Library manuscript (Add. MS. 10444), but there is no certainty that it belongs with Shakespeare's play. It was more likely to have been intended for a 'tempest' dance in a court masque and so is not reprinted here.

1. 'FULL FATHOM FIVE' (I.2.396).

Full fa-thom five thy fa - ther lies, Of his bones are cor - al made; Those are pearls that were his eyes; No-thing of him that doth fade But doth suf-fer a sea change In - to some thing rich and strange. Sea-nymphs hour-ly ring his knell. Hark, now I hear them, Hark, now I hear them, ding dong bell. Ding dong, ding dong bell. Ding dong, ding dong bell. Ding dong, ding dong bell.

2. 'WHERE THE BEE SUCKS' (V.i.88).

Commentary

F refers to the first Folio (1623). Quotations from other plays by Shakespeare are taken from the Penguin Shakespeare series.

The Characters in the Play

Sebastian, Antonio and Ferdinand were common Italian names, though Shakespeare might have found them together in William Thomas's *History of Italy* (1549), a book which also discusses a Duke of Genoa called Prospero Adorno. The name Alonso is a Spanish form of Alfonso. Two famous kings of Naples were called Alfonso, and a triumphal arch celebrating Alfonso I's entry in 1443 still stands in the city today. The name Prospero turns up in Ben Jonson's *Every Man in his Humour* (1598), a play in which Shakespeare is known to have acted. The Latin adjective *prospero* means 'favourable, propitious, prospering'. Trinculo's name probably derives from the Italian *trincare*, 'to drink greedily'.

The names Miranda and Caliban were invented by Shakespeare. Miranda derives from the Italian *mirando*, 'wondrous', or from its Latin root *miror*, 'to admire or wonder at': Ferdinand calls her 'Admired Miranda' at III.1.37. Caliban may be a kind of anagram of 'cannibal', or may relate to the place-names Calibia in North Africa, or Caribana in South America, which appear on some sixteenth-century maps. Other less persuasive derivations have been proposed, including the Arabic *kalebon* (vile dog), and the Romany *caulibon* (dark thing). Ariel's name was probably chosen for its association with the air, in contrast to Caliban's earthiness

(cf. *thou, which art but air* V.1.21). The Elizabethan magus John
Dee communicated with a spirit called Uriel; there is also an angel
named Uriel in the Jewish cabbala. In one passage of the Bible
(Isaiah 29), the city of Jerusalem is called Ariel, a name which is
glossed in the Geneva Bible (1560) as meaning 'lion of God'.
Perhaps this association feeds into Ariel's performance as the
terrifying harpy in III.3.

Since this list groups Ariel with Miranda and the other female
characters, who would have been played by boy actors, it seems
likely that in Shakespeare's theatre Ariel was also played by a
boy. This helps to explain his rather androgynous, gender-
indeterminate quality. Masculine pronouns are used of him at
I.2.193 and in the stage directions at III.3.52 and 82, but when he
wears disguises, they are always female: a *nymph o' th' sea* (I.2.301),
a *harpy* (III.3.52) and *Ceres* (IV.1.60). In performances from the
eighteenth to the mid twentieth century, Ariel was always played
by female actors, and only in recent times has the part typically
been taken by a man. When played by a woman, Ariel's parallels
with Miranda as well as Caliban become more apparent.

I.1

The setting is a ship at sea, the only scene in the play not located
on the 'uninhabited island' specified at the end of the list of characters. In Shakespeare's theatre, thunder was produced by rolling
a cannonball in the roof over the stage, or with a drum. Lightning
could be made with fireworks, though the opening stage direction only calls for offstage noise, probably because fireworks would
not have been used in performances at the Blackfriars, a small
roofed playhouse.

    1 *Boatswain*: Pronounced 'bosun'.

    2 *What cheer*: How are you?

    3 *Good*: I.e. 'good sir' or 'good fellow'. The word is used
       several times in this scene as a form of address.
       yarely: Briskly (a nautical term).

    4 *Bestir*: Get moving.
       Enter Mariners: F's stage directions are defective in this
       scene and make no attempt to convey its busy action.
       Although the Mariners are marked to enter here
       and again – *wet* – at 49, there is no intervening exit

direction for them. In most productions, the Mariners move about the stage throughout the dialogue, conveying the violence of the storm through chaotic action, and this is probably what happened in Shakespeare's theatre.

5 *Cheerly*: With a will.

6 *topsail*: The highest sail on the main mast.

  Tend: Listen carefully. The whistle was used by ships' masters to direct the crew's actions, such as the taking in of sails commanded here.

7–8 *Blow till thou burst thy wind, if room enough*: Blow as hard as you like, so long as we have sufficient space in which to manoeuvre.

10 *Play the men*: Act like men.

13 *Do you not hear him*: Can't you hear his whistle (offstage).

14 *You do assist the storm*: By getting in the way of the Mariners.

16 *cares*: In Elizabethan English, a singular verb with a plural subject was a permissible usage. Cf. III.3.2, *aches*, one of many similar instances in this play.

17 *roarers*: Waves. At this time 'roarers' was also used as slang meaning 'riotous, unruly or quarrelsome people', so here it gives an impression of social collapse as well as physical danger.

21 *these elements*: The winds and waves.

22 *work the peace of the present*: Make the present moment peaceful, by calming the storm – if you can do such a thing on your own authority (a sarcastic remark).

23 *hand*: Handle.

28–30 *Methinks ... gallows*: Gonzalo alludes to the proverb 'He that is born to be hanged shall never be drowned', making grim humour out of a desperate situation; *complexion* means the man's character, as seen in his face.

31 *rope of his destiny*: Hangman's cord; but the Fates (destinies) were also spoken of as spinning the thread of man's life.

32 *doth little advantage*: Is little help.

34 *topmast*: Upper section of the main mast.

35 *Bring her to try with main-course*: Put her under the mainsail, with the other sails tightly furled. The Boatswain
is attempting to keep the boat manoeuvrable, while
reducing her speed. His language is taken from the technical vocabulary of seventeenth-century seamanship.

36 *A plague*: F has a dash after this word, which may indicate the excision of some profanity, especially as
mention is later made of the Boatswain's ripe language
(V.1.218–19). Perhaps the copyist or printer censored
Shakespeare's text. However, religious oaths were
forbidden by statute on the Jacobean stage, and the
Boatswain never actually says anything offensive –
though he is very insulting towards the aristocrats, and
Sebastian calls him 'blasphemous' (40–41). In the text
as we have it, Antonio and Sebastian swear more than
he does.

37 *or our office*: Or than we are in our work. The Boatswain
complains that the passengers' exclamations are noisier
than the storm and make it hard to hear the Master's
whistle.

45 *warrant him for drowning*: Guarantee he won't drown.

46–7 *leaky as an unstanched wench*: A piece of casual
misogyny, comparing the ship to a woman, who is
herself like a barrel that has not been properly sealed
(*unstanched*). The notion that women were *leaky* was
proverbial at this time, either because women's bodies
were associated with watery fluids such as tears, milk
and menstrual blood, or because of assumptions about
women's supposed sexual uncontrollability.

48 *Lay her a-hold*: Bring the ship close to the wind.
Set her two courses: Set out the foresail as well as the
mainsail (in order to bring the ship into open sea).

51 *must our mouths be cold*: Must we die? Some editors
believe that the Boatswain is asking for a drink to
drown his sorrows, for Antonio calls the Mariners
drunkards at 54. But Antonio is an unsympathetic
witness, and the sailors have shown themselves more
courageous than the courtiers.

54 *merely*: Utterly.

55 *wide-chopped*: Big-mouthed.
56 *ten tides*: Pirates were hanged on shore at the low-water
    mark, and their bodies left there until three tides had
    washed over them. Antonio characteristically increases
    the number to ten.
58 *glut*: Swallow.
59–60 *We split . . . we split*: Although F prints these lines as
    verse, they are probably meant to be shouted out in no
    particular order.
63 *heath*: Heather.
    furze: Gorse.

I.2

The setting shifts to Prospero's island, where it remains for the
rest of the play. This long, complex scene is constructed as a
series of conversations between Prospero and members of his
'family', which supply the various back-stories to the play's action.
Prospero's voice is dominant, but by characterizing Ariel and
Caliban vividly, and allowing them to contest Prospero's account
of events, Shakespeare permits us to see that there is more than
one perspective from which the action can be viewed.

Prospero enters wearing his magic cloak, which embodies his
supernatural power (*my art*, 25) and which he takes off (at 24) in
order to talk to Miranda on more equal terms. Probably he also
carries a magic staff: his *stick* is mentioned at 472 (see also V.1.54).
There is, of course, a surprise for the audience in this revelation
of Prospero's magic. The storm which seemed so real in scene 1
is disclosed in scene 2 as having been produced by his art.

 1 *art*: Magic power.
 2 *allay*: Quieten.
 4 *But that*: Were it not that.
    th'welkin's cheek: The face of the sky.
 6 *brave*: Fine.
11 *or ere*: Before.
13 *fraughting souls*: People being carried (like cargo).
    Be collected: Compose yourself.
14 *piteous*: Pitiful.
18–19 *naught knowing | Of whence I am*: Knowing nothing
    about where I came from.

19 *more better*: Of higher status (the double comparative was acceptable grammar in Shakespeare's day).

20 *full poor cell*: Very humble dwelling (cf. Friar Lawrence's 'cell' in *Romeo and Juliet*, II.2.192).

22 *meddle*: Mingle.

25 *my art*: Prospero addresses his cloak.

26 *direful*: Dreadful.

27 *virtue*: Essence.

28 *provision*: Foresight.

29–32 *that there is no soul ... which thou saw'st sink*: In re-assuring Miranda that no one has been harmed in the storm, Prospero corrects himself: not even the hair of anyone's head has been hurt. Cf. 217: *Not a hair perished*.

30 *perdition*: Loss.

31 *Betid*: Happened.

32 *Which thou heard'st cry ... saw'st sink*: The first 'which' refers to the passengers, the second to the vessel itself.

35 *bootless inquisition*: Fruitless inquiry.

41 *Out*: Fully.

43–4 *that | Hath kept with thy remembrance*: That you can recall; that remains (like an image) in your memory.

45–6 *an assurance | That my remembrance warrants*: A certainty that my memory knows for sure.

47 *tended*: Attended.

50 *backward*: Past portion (of time). Shakespeare here uses the adjective 'backward' as if it were a noun, the first such usage recorded.
abysm: Abyss.

54 *Milan*: Accented on the first syllable.

56–7 *Thy mother ... thou wast my daughter*: Prospero pays tribute to the fidelity of his dead wife (*piece* here means 'masterpiece'). However, his attempt at humour – joking that Miranda must be his child because his wife was always faithful to him – seems rather insensitive, and anticipates the anxieties that he voices elsewhere about female sexuality.

58 *his only heir*: By emphasizing that he has no other children, Prospero underlines that Miranda is the political heir to Milan as well as his daughter. This makes the

choice of a husband for her a very delicate matter. In introducing her to Ferdinand, the heir to the kingdom of Naples, Prospero is not only matchmaking but engaging in high-level diplomacy.

59 *no worse issued*: Of no meaner birth.

63 *holp*: Helped.

64 *teen*: Grief.

65 *from my remembrance*: Outside my recollection.

66–74 *My brother ... a parallel*: The syntax of Prospero's speech is very confused, expressing the complexity of the events he has to describe, and the pain he still feels at them. He begins to recount Antonio's treachery, but has to interrupt himself to fill in details he omitted to explain about the dignity of Milan, and his own reputation as Duke.

68–9 *whom next thyself | Of all the world I loved*: Whom, after you, I loved most of all in the whole world.

69–70 *put | The manage*: Entrusted the administration.

71 *signories*: Italian lordships.

72 *prime*: Senior.

73 *liberal arts*: Subjects studied at Renaissance universities, and to which, Prospero says, he devoted himself: grammar, logic, rhetoric, arithmetic, geometry, music and astronomy – though *secret studies* (77) suggests he focused on magic and the occult.

75 *cast*: Bestowed.

76 *my state*: My dukedom.
    transported: Enraptured.

78 *Dost thou attend me*: Are you paying attention? Prospero's sharp rebukes, here and subsequently, do not mean that Miranda is inattentive or even sleepy. They reflect his own anxiety about the story he tells, his need to describe it fully, and convey the resentment that he still feels towards Alonso and Antonio. This is necessary to give significance to his eventual decision to forgive his enemies rather than take revenge (V.1.25–30).

79 *perfected*: Fully skilled in.

79–81 *how to grant suits ... trash for over-topping*: Prospero

offers a succinct summary of the modern techniques
of courtly power, such as were in vogue in the
Renaissance amongst those readers of Machiavelli who
understood politics as the art of the possible; *suits* are
the requests addressed to princes for favour, help or
reward. Antonio has learned that a good way of keeping
his subjects dependent on him is arbitrarily to fulfil
their requests on some occasions but refuse them on
others. So too, he has promoted some followers, but
trashed others for *over-topping* (i.e. put them down when
they became too powerful): this suggests that he exer-
cised authority ruthlessly and with a deliberate artfulness; *trash* is a term from hunting, meaning 'to rein in
a dog'.

82 *The creatures that were mine*: My former servants, officers
or dependants: those people whom Prospero 'created'
by rewards and promotions, but whom Antonio *new
created* (81) by granting favours and honours that
diverted their loyalties from him.

83 *key*: The initial sense is 'the keys of office', but the
image develops into that of a key in music: all now
sing to Antonio's tune.

87 *verdure*: Sap, vitality. Prospero imagines himself as a
tree being strangled by Antonio's *ivy* (86).

89–90 *dedicated | To closeness*: Devoted to seclusion.

91–2 *that which . . . all popular rate*: Two ideas are combined
here: that although Prospero's studies led him to neglect
his worldly business, they were of greater value than
the people esteemed them to be; and that Prospero's
studies, by their very abstruseness, put him at a distance
from his people. It is difficult to disentangle these over-
lapping meanings with complete confidence. Either
way, Prospero suggests that, being distracted by his
art, he allowed Antonio the opportunity of seizing
power for himself.

94–5 *Like a good parent, did beget of him | A falsehood*:
Prospero alludes to the paradoxical proverb 'Trust is
the mother of deceit'. As Miranda will say, *Good wombs
have borne bad sons* (120).

97   *sans bound*: Without limit.
     lorded: Endowed with lordship.

98   *revenue*: Accented on the second syllable.

100–102 *having into truth ... credit his own lie*: I.e. Antonio himself came to take for a truth what first he had told as a lie; *into* here has the sense of 'unto' or 'against'.

103 *out o'th'substitution*: As a consequence of acting as my substitute.

104 *executing th'outward face of royalty*: Performing the exterior appearance of legitimate power.

105 *prerogative*: Rights and privileges of rule.

107–8 *To have no screen ... him he played it for*: To eliminate any difference between being the duke himself and merely playing the role on behalf of someone else (i.e. Prospero).

109 *Absolute Milan*: Absolute sovereign of Milan.

111 *confederates*: Enters into confederacy.

112 *dry*: Thirsty.

113 *annual tribute*: Yearly rent (cf. II.1.293).

114 *Subject his coronet to his crown*: As King of Naples, Alonso governs a large and powerful territory in southern Italy, whereas Milan, though a great northern state, is still merely a dukedom. There is thus a significant hierarchy between the princes in the play, which helps to explain why Prospero is so keen to marry his daughter to Alonso's son. In fact, at the time when Shakespeare wrote the play, both Milan and Naples were satellite states of Spain.

115 *yet unbowed*: Hitherto free and independent.

117 *his condition and th'event*: His pact (with Naples) and its outcome.

118–19 *I should sin | To think but nobly of my grandmother*: A backhanded compliment to Prospero's mother (cf. 56–7 and note). Antonio's evil makes Miranda wonder momentarily whether he really could have been her father's legitimate brother.

123 *in lieu o'th'premises*: In return for the pledge.

125 *presently*: At once.
     extirpate: Uproot.

129 *Fated*: Destined by fate.

131 *ministers for th'purpose*: Agents employed.

134 *hint*: Occasion.

135 *wrings*: Forces.

138 *impertinent*: Irrelevant.

142 *mark*: Sign, literally 'signature'.

143 *colours*: Appearances (punning on the *bloody* mark).

144 *In few*: Briefly.
     barque: Small boat.

146 *butt*: Tub, here used metaphorically for a poor vessel.

148 *hoist us*: Lifted us up.

149-50 *To cry to th'sea ... sighing back again*: Prospero inten-
     sifies his narrative – which thus far has been terse and
     urgent – by embellishing it with poetic fancies. He
     ascribes to the sea and wind feelings of pity for him
     and Miranda: their roaring and blowing is imagined as
     sympathetically echoing the castaways' cries and sighs.

151 *loving wrong*: I.e. the winds harmed us, by blowing us
     out to sea, but pitied us as they did so.

152 *cherubin*: Guardian angel.

155 *decked*: Covered, literally 'adorned, ornamented'.

156 *which*: Miranda's smiling.

157 *undergoing stomach*: Spirit of endurance.

159 *By providence divine*: Like most editors, I have strength-
     ened the punctuation in F (which reads *divine,*). F's
     comma creates a different syntax, so that Prospero says
     it was by *providence* (good foresight) that they happened
     to have provisions in their boat. However, his three
     words seem more properly to be an answer to Miranda's
     question (*How came we ashore?*), and hence to voice the
     more extravagant claim that they survived because they
     were protected by supernatural power.

163 *design*: Project.

164 *stuffs*: Household goods.

165 *steaded much*: Been very useful.

169 *Now I arise*: Probably Prospero stands, and resumes his
     magic cloak, ready to charm Miranda asleep and to call
     Ariel.

173 *Than other princes can*: Than other princesses can have

(at this time 'princes' was used indifferently to mean
royal children of either sex).

174 *careful*: Diligent.

180 *prescience*: Foresight.

181 *zenith*: High point of good fortune; an astrological term,
referring to the orbit of the *star* (182) which influences
Prospero's life.

183 *omit*: Neglect.

185 *dullness*: Drowsiness.

186 *give it way*: Give in to it.

192 *task*: Assign work to.

193 *quality*: Companion spirits.

194 *to point*: Exactly.

196 *beak*: Prow.

197 *waist*: The ship's middle.

198 *flamed amazement*: Ariel indicates that he appeared to
the mariners like a flame, something which associates
him with St Elmo's fire, the strange electrical phenomenon often observed at sea.

200 *yards*: Crossbars on the masts.
     bowsprit: Boom extending from the bow, to which the
     jib is fixed.
     distinctly: Separately.

201 *Jove's*: Jove was king of the Roman gods, whose power
was manifested in his control of the thunder.

202 *momentary*: Lasting only a moment.

203 *sight out-running*: Moving faster than the eye can
follow.

204 *Neptune*: God of the sea (who carried a three-pronged
trident).

207 *coil*: Tumult.

209 *fever of the mad*: Fever such as madmen feel.

213 *up-staring*: Standing on end.

218 *sustaining garments*: Probably the Neapolitans' clothes
were *sustaining* because air trapped inside them kept
them afloat in the water. Shakespeare uses a similar
conceit in relation to the drowning Ophelia in *Hamlet*
(IV.7.175–6): 'Her clothes spread wide, | And
mermaid-like awhile they bore her up.'

220 *troops*: Separate groups.

223 *odd angle*: Remote corner.

224 *this sad knot*: Ariel folds his arms, in demonstration to Prospero. Such a posture, and sighing, was the conventional sign of melancholy.

228 *dew*: Used in magical potions; cf. 321.

229 *still-vexed*: Always angry.

Bermudas: Islands in the north Atlantic, so not part of the play's Mediterranean geography. The Bermudas (discovered in 1515) were notorious amongst mariners for their storminess; they had to be skirted by ships coming northwards from the Caribbean in search of the westerly winds that would take them home. William Strachey, who was wrecked here in 1609, called them 'dangerous and dreaded' (see Introduction, pp. xxvi–xxvii).

231 *their suffered labour*: The toil they have undergone.

234 *float*: Sea, a figurative use; literally 'tide'.

239–40 *Past the mid-season.* | *At least two glasses*: Two hours after midday (measured by hourglasses).

240 *'twixt six and now*: This play is unusual in that it happens in real time, its events taking exactly as long to happen as time passes in the theatre. Performances on Shakespeare's stage began at 2 p.m. and ran for three or four hours.

241 *preciously*: As a precious thing.

243 *remember*: Remind.

244 *Moody*: Angry, obstinate.

249 *or . . . or*: Either . . . or.

250 *bate me*: Reduce my term of service. Ariel is an indentured servant to Prospero, whose work is usually spoken of in terms similar to an apprenticeship, to run for a fixed period. By contrast, Caliban is spoken of simply as a *slave* (though Prospero does once apply this word to Ariel, at 270).

253 *salt deep*: Seabed.

255 *veins o'th'earth*: Underground streams.

256 *baked*: Hardened.

257 *malignant*: Rebellious.

258 *Sycorax*: A name invented by Shakespeare, possibly
    derived from the Greek words *sus* (sow) and *korax*
    (raven). There may be an association with the classical
    witch Medea, who was called the 'Scythian raven' (for
    Medea's lurking presence in the play, see note to
    V.1.33–50). Alternatively, the derivation could be from
    the Coraxi tribe in Colchis, the birthplace of another
    famous classical witch, Circe. These associations extend
    Sycorax's significance as a witch beyond her local birth-
    place in Algiers.

259 *grown into a hoop*: I.e. bent over, so that her chin met
    her knees.

261 *Algiers*: In North Africa, 400 miles east of Tunis; spelled
    Argier in F. A vassal state of the Ottoman empire,
    Algiers was the principal base of the Barbary pirates.
    The emperor Charles V failed to capture it in 1541.

266 *one thing she did*: Usually explained as Sycorax's preg-
    nancy, which would have saved her from hanging,
    though a woman with child could be executed after she
    had given birth. There is also a story that the Spanish
    siege of Algiers in 1541 was destroyed by a storm raised
    by a witch.

269 *blue-eyed*: Usually explained as 'with blue eyelids',
    which at this time were taken as a sign of pregnancy.
    Some editors think the blue is meant pejoratively, since
    it was the colour of envy, or was sometimes associated
    with old, malevolent women. Alternatively, it could be
    a printer's mistake for 'blear-eyed'; or it could mean
    that Sycorax, though ugly, was in other ways powerful
    and compelling, an unsettling mix of the repellent and
    the desirable.

272 *for*: Because.

272–4 *for thou wast ... Refusing her grand hests*: Sycorax's
    magic was powerful enough to draw Ariel into her
    service, but not to make him perform commands (*hests*)
    that went against his nature – much the same problem,
    in fact, that Prospero has with him.

275 *ministers*: Spirits.

276 *unmitigable*: Unassuageable.

281 *As fast as millwheels strike*: As frequently as each blade of a millwheel hits the water.

282 *litter*: Give birth to (used of animal births).

283 *whelp*: This term is usually applied to a dog's young, though in the next line Prospero admits Caliban is of *human shape*.

287–9 *Thy groans . . . ever-angry bears*: Ariel's torments were such that they aroused a sympathetic response even in creatures conventionally regarded as savage.

292 *made gape*: Opened up.

294 *more murmur'st*: Complain again.

295 *his knotty entrails*: Its gnarled inner parts.

297 *correspondent*: Submissive.

301 *make thyself like to a nymph o'th'sea*: It is odd that Prospero requires Ariel to take this disguise, when immediately afterwards he commands him to be invisible. Presumably it is for the benefit of the theatre audience, who are shortly to see Ariel like a sea-nymph leading Ferdinand from the ocean.

307 *Heaviness*: Drowsiness.

309 *villain*: Low-born person (technically 'villein', a peasant).

311 *miss*: Do without. Some readers have felt it to be a contradiction that Prospero needs Caliban's labour, when his magic is in other respects so powerful. But Prospero's magic does not consist of demonic help (such as Dr Faustus has) or conjuring tricks. A distinction is maintained between the menial tasks that Caliban performs – fetching wood, catching fish, cleaning plates (see II.2.180–82) – and the activities of Ariel and his spirits, which involve controlling the elements and producing music and mental illusions. Prospero uses his power over spirits to effect his purposes in the material world, but not as a short cut to ease and convenience. The importance and necessity of physical labour is insisted on in III.1.

312 *offices*: Tasks.

318 *Hark in thine ear*: Prospero instructs Ariel to fetch Ferdinand.

319 *got by the devil himself*: In European witch-beliefs, it was supposed that witches commonly had intercourse with the devil.

320 *dam*: Mother (normally used of animals).

321 *wicked dew*: Cf. 228 and note.

322 *raven's feather*: The raven was a bird associated with witches (see note to 258).

323 *southwest*: A south-west wind – warm, damp and unwholesome.

326 *pen thy breath up*: Prevent you from breathing freely.
    urchins: Spirits in the shape of hedgehogs.

327 *for that vast of night that they may work*: For that long period of darkness when evil spirits can walk abroad.

328–9 *pinched | As thick as honeycomb*: Given pinch marks as dense as cells in a honeycomb.

331 *This island's mine*: Modern interpretations that see Prospero as a kind of colonizer and Caliban as a displaced native have taken this claim as central to the play: see Introduction, pp. xlvii–xlviii.

335 *the bigger light, and . . . the less*: The sun and the moon (an echo of Genesis 1:16).

338 *brine-pits*: Salty springs; Caliban showed Prospero the island's bad *qualities* as well as good.

342 *sty me*: Pen me up.

345 *stripes*: Lashes.

351–62 *Abhorrèd slave . . . more than a prison*: In many editions and productions this speech has been transferred to Prospero, on the presumption that its harshness of expression makes it inappropriate for Miranda. It is true that such slips occasionally arise in F, for the speech-prefixes also need correcting at II.1.38–9. However, in this instance the desire for change seems to owe more to modern notions about appropriate female behaviour than they do to any manifest textual error. Caliban's reply, *You taught me language*, is addressed to Miranda, as is confirmed by his later remark that she taught him about the moon (II.2.139–40).

352 *print*: Imprint.

358 *race*: Inherited disposition, inborn qualities.

362 *more than a prison*: A worse punishment (i.e. death).

364 *red plague*: Plague that produces red sores.
      rid: Destroy.

365 *Hag-seed*: Witch's offspring.

366 *thou'rt best*: You had better (do so).

369 *old cramps*: Pains such as old people have.

370 *aches*: Pronounced 'aitches'.
      make thee roar: As Sycorax made Ariel suffer.

373 *Setebos*: The name of a Patagonian devil, mentioned
      in an early narrative of Magellan's expedition to South
      America, collected and translated in Robert Eden's
      History of Travel (1577).

374 *playing and singing*: In Shakespeare's theatre, Ariel
      probably accompanied himself on the lute.

377 *Curtsied when you have, and kissed*: Curtseying and kiss-
      ing hands were the customary gestures at the start of a
      dance. Some editors omit the comma at the end of the
      line and take *kissed* as referring to the *waves*, so that the
      kissing of the dancers itself stills the waves into silence.

378 *whist*: Hush.

379 *featly*: Nimbly.

383 *Burden, dispersedly*: Refrain, from around the stage.
      This was probably sung by the *sprites* that Ariel sings
      of in 380. Some may have been in the music room over
      the stage: Ferdinand hears music *above me* at 407. The
      layout of the song in F is very confusing, and makes
      it hard to be sure which words are the refrain and when
      the refrain was sung. (The printer's arrangement was
      dictated by the limitations of the columns on the page,
      rather than fidelity to the song's musical shape: see
      Collation 1.) The rearrangement adopted in this edition
      assumes that the refrain was simply 'Bow-wow, bow-
      wow', but other options are possible: perhaps the sprites
      sang 381–3, or 383 and 386.

385 *chanticleer*: A poetical name for a cockerel, and specif-
      ically given to the boastful cock in Chaucer's *Nun's
      Priest's Tale*.

388 *waits*: Attends.

390 *again*: Repeatedly.

392 *passion*: Grief.

393 *air*: Tune.

396 *Full fathom five*: At least thirty feet deep. 'The sea-change of which Ariel sings, the transmutation of the body of Ferdinand's father into substances "rich and strange", makes this death suddenly unreal and without pain. It allows Ferdinand to turn his whole mind to Miranda, almost at once, without seeming callous or heedless of his loss' (Anne Barton, 1968 edition).

399 *fade*: Decay.

404 *Ding, dong*: As in the previous song, the refrain is taken up by the spirits. A contemporary setting of this song survives by the lutenist Robert Johnson (see The Music). In Johnson's version, the words 'Ding, dong bell' are extended into an imitative canon.

405 *remember*: Recall.

407 *owes*: Owns.

408 *The fringèd curtains of thine eye advance*: Raise your eyelids. Prospero moves into a higher rhetorical gear for Miranda's encounter with Ferdinand.

411 *brave*: Handsome.

414 *but*: Except that.

415 *canker*: (1) Cankerworm; (2) corrosive.

418 *nothing natural*: Nothing in the realm of nature.

421 *Most sure, the goddess*: An echo of Aeneas's words on meeting with his mother Venus in Virgil's *Aeneid*, I.328: 'O dea certe.'

422 *airs*: Songs.

423 *remain*: Dwell.

425 *bear*: Conduct.

426 *you wonder*: Ferdinand unknowingly intuits Miranda's name, which is derived from the Latin *miror*, 'to wonder'.

427 *If you be maid or no*: Whether you are a mortal or a goddess.

429–30 *I am the best ... where 'tis spoken*: Believing that his father has drowned, Ferdinand alludes to his new status as King of Naples. His next speech continues to play cryptically with the idea that he now embodies his father.

432 *single*: Solitary, lonely.

433 *He does hear me*: I, being King of Naples, hear myself.

435 *at ebb*: At low tide (i.e. tearless).

438 *his brave son*: Nowhere else in the play is it suggested that Antonio (the present Duke of Milan) has a son. Some editors see this as a sign that the text we have has lost some material through theatrical cuts, but it is more likely that Shakespeare changed his mind as he wrote into the play, or just forgot about this detail (as, with minor characters, he sometimes did). By the time we reach II.1.111–12, where Alonso calls his son *mine heir | Of Naples and of Milan*, the expectation is clearly that Ferdinand would inherit both territories, so that in the next generation Milan will be entirely absorbed by Naples. Of course, it would radically alter the end of the play were Antonio to have a child. It is important that Miranda should be the sole heir of Milan, and that no one else is around who might dispute her inheritance.

439 *more braver*: More excellent.
    control: Contradict.

441 *changed eyes*: Fallen in love.

443 *done yourself some wrong*: Fallen into an error (in believing yourself King).

447 *if a virgin*: If you are unmarried.

451 *uneasy*: Difficult.

451–2 *lest too light winning | Make the prize light*: In case obtaining the prize (Miranda) too easily makes her value seem too little (to Ferdinand). There's also a hint that if Ferdinand does not offer marriage, he will make Miranda 'light', i.e. a whore.

454 *ow'st*: Owns.

457–9 *There's nothing ill . . . will strive to dwell with't*: Miranda advances the conventional Neoplatonic idea that exterior beauty is a sign of inner moral purity, and anticipates the objection that outsides are no guides to insides: even if so lovely a body contained an *ill spirit*, its beauty would draw good things to it.

463 *fresh-brook mussels*: River mussels (an inedible variety).

465 *entertainment*: Treatment.

467 *rash*: Hasty.

468 *gentle, and not fearful*: High born, and not cowardly.

469 *My foot my tutor*: How dare the foot – a lowly part of
the body – attempt to instruct the head?

471 *ward*: Posture of defence.

472 *this stick*: Prospero's magic staff.

475 *surety*: Guarantee.

478 *shapes as he*: Humans shaped like him.

480 *To*: Compared to.

484 *nerves*: Sinews.

488 *nor this man's threats*: Here 'nor' takes the sense of
'and', but syntactically it creates an implied comparison: 'neither these various disasters, nor Prospero's
threats mean anything to me, if I can see Miranda once
a day.'

491 *All corners else*: Everywhere else.

492 *liberty*: People who are free.

495 *Hark what thou else shalt do me*: Prospero draws Ariel
aside, giving Miranda and Ferdinand a brief private
moment.

497 *unwonted*: Unusual.

499 *then*: Till then.

II.1

In this complex opening conversation, Gonzalo and Adrian try
to comfort Alonso, contriving sallies of polite discourse on topics
provoked by their current experiences which attempt to uphold
the normality of court life in the face of abnormal events.
Meanwhile, Antonio and Sebastian make sarcastic fun out of their
well-meaning but ineffective consolations. Probably they stand
slightly apart from the main group, as sometimes their interrup-
tions are unheard by the rest, sometimes not. At other times the
King's party keep their dignity by simply pretending not to hear
them.

0 *and others*: Here, and elsewhere (I.1.8, III.3.0), the stage
directions allow for an unspecified number of silent
courtiers to swell the scene. It is impossible to be sure
whether these instructions came from Shakespeare or
were added in by the scribe who copied his manuscript.

Some editors delete them, but they are left here since
'permissive' directions are common in early play-texts.

2–3 *our escape | Is much beyond our loss*: Our good fortune
in surviving far exceeds what we have lost.

3 *hint*: Occasion.

5 *The masters of some merchant, and the merchant*: The
officers of some merchant vessel, and her owner.

11 *cold porridge*: Sebastian makes a poor pun on Alonso's
peace, which sounds like 'pease', an ingredient of
porridge.

12 *visitor*: Comforter; a member of the parish charged with
visiting the sick.

17 *One: tell*: Gonzalo's wit has struck one – keep count.

18 *when every grief is entertained that's offered*: If a person
embraces every cause of grief that presents itself.

20 *A dollar*: Sebastian pretends *entertainer* must mean 'inn-
keeper', who could be paid with this German coin.
Gonzalo's riposte recovers his original meaning by
taking *dollar* as 'dolour', sorrow.

26 *spendthrift*: Waster.

27 *spare*: Stop.

37 *desert*: Uninhabited.

38–9 *Ha, ha, ha. | So, you're paid*: Antonio laughs because
he has won the bet, the *cockerel* (Adrian) having broken
silence before the *old cock* (Gonzalo), and Sebastian
acknowledges his victory: *you're paid*. In F the speech-
prefixes for these lines are the wrong way around; such
a slip could easily have been made either by the copyist
or the printer.

43 *He could not miss't*: He had to say that.

45 *temperance*: Mild climate (taken by Antonio in the next
line as a girl's name).

51 *fen*: Marsh.

57 *an eye of green*: A touch of green.

58 *He misses not much*: He's not far wrong (ironical).

61 *credit*: Belief.

62 *vouched rarities*: Guaranteed oddities.

65 *gloss*: Lustre.

69 *or very falsely pocket up his report*: Gonzalo's pocket

would suppress his idea by hiding it away, because he is so totally wrong. In fact, Gonzalo has pointed out something to which Antonio and Sebastian are wilfully blind: as Ariel says, their garments have been left 'fresher than before' (I.2.219).

72 *Tunis*: A city in north Africa, now the capital of Tunisia. It was held by the Spanish in 1535–69 and 1573–4 but subsequently became a province of the Ottoman empire.

77 *Dido*: A mythical queen of Carthage, an ancient north African city. Today the remains of Dido's Carthage stand seven miles outside Tunis: Gonzalo and Adrian pedantically disagree over whether ancient Carthage and modern Tunis are one and the same (83–6). Dido was a *widow* because she inherited her power on the death of her husband, Sychaeus, who founded the city. In one version of her story, she commits suicide rather than marry an African king, a parallel which draws attention to the distaste that Claribel feels for her marriage. In a different, more developed version told by Virgil in Books I–IV of *The Aeneid*, her story is entwined with that of Aeneas, the founder of Rome. After the sack of Troy, Virgil's Aeneas journeys into exile with his followers to find a site for a new kingdom, but is driven ashore at Carthage by a storm. There he falls in love with Dido, but abandons her when the gods command him to resume his search for Rome; Dido commits suicide out of despair at his betrayal. Modern readers of *The Tempest* often find the discussion of Dido opaque, but her famous tale acts as a shadow behind the play's action, as its characters are following the same route between north Africa and Italy, and are subject to similar storms and destinies. The tragedy of Virgil's Dido was that Aeneas betrayed her love for the sake of his political ambitions, a danger that perhaps motivates Prospero's protective feelings towards Miranda. At the same time, the marriage of Ferdinand's sister Claribel to an African prince is an act of dynastic miscegenation of a kind which the more eurocentric

Aeneas considered but ultimately turned away from.

80 *widower Aeneas*: Aeneas had in fact lost his first wife in the fall of Troy.

87 *the miraculous harp*: In Greek myth, the sound of Amphion's harp miraculously caused stones to erect themselves into the walls of Thebes. Gonzalo has done more than this, by creating houses as well as walls.

95 *Why, in good time*: Antonio reacts to Gonzalo suddenly speaking after several lines' silence. In F Gonzalo's *Ay* (94) is printed as *I*, and is usually modernized as in this edition. Perhaps, though, 'I –' should be retained as a false start to his next remark.

99 *And the rarest that e'er came there*: A sardonic echo of Adrian's words at 75–6.

100 *Bate*: Except.

103 *in a sort*: After a fashion.

106–7 *against | The stomach of my sense*: In opposition to my appetite. Alonso complains he is being force-fed trivial conversation which he does not wish to hear.

109 *rate*: Judgement.

113–22 *Sir, he may live ... alive to land*: Aside from three words at III.3.40, this is Francisco's only speech, and some editors take Antonio's remark at 231–5, that Gonzalo has striven to persuade Alonso that his son still lives, as the basis for reassigning these lines. It's possible that in writing the play Shakespeare did not know how many spare actors he had to swell out Alonso's court, and changed his mind as the scene went on. Still, the neutrality of Francisco's identity makes his words about Ferdinand's heroism all the more trustworthy. His character has not been sabotaged by comments from the cynics, and his language has an epic resonance unlike that used by Gonzalo. It has been suggested that this account of Ferdinand's swimming draws on a description of sea-serpents in Virgil's *Aeneid*, II.203–8.

118 *contentious*: Quarrelsome.

120–21 *th'shore, that o'er his wave-worn ... to relieve him*: The cliffs to which Ferdinand swims have been eroded at

the base, and appear to lean forward as if to aid him.
In these lines, *his* (as often) means 'its'.

125 *loose her*: F is ambiguous, since *loose* was also a seventeenth-century spelling of the modern word 'lose', and
some editors print that. Either spelling is defensible,
though 'loose' is more resonant, implying that Alonso
recklessly gave away his authority over Claribel, or
that he 'let her loose' (with an underlying sexual conno-
tation). The alternative, that Alonso merely 'lose[s]'
Claribel to his son-in-law, makes him seem curiously
passive, as though it was not his choice; and it redun-
dantly repeats *this great loss* (123; also cf. 135).

127 *hath cause to wet the grief on't*: Has reason to weep at
this lamentable situation.

130 *Weighed between loathness and obedience*: Claribel was
torn between dislike of the marriage and duty to her
father's will. The image is of a pair of scales, with a
beam tilting one way or the other.

132–4 *Milan and Naples ... to comfort them*: Sebastian means
that even if the survivors get home, they will be
outnumbered by the men who have drowned in the
voyage.

135 *dear'st o'th'loss*: Heaviest losses. Alonso takes the blame,
but has suffered the most.

138 *And time to speak it in*: I.e. now's not the time to appor-
tion blame.

140 *chirurgeonly*: Like a surgeon.

143 *Had I plantation of this isle*: Gonzalo means, if I had
the task of colonizing the island; in 144, Antonio parodies his 'plantation' by taking it to mean 'cultivation'.

144 *nettle-seed ... docks, or mallows*: Weeds.

146 *want*: Lack.

147–64 *I'th'commonwealth ... my innocent people*: Gonzalo's
remarkable speech, about the perfect state that could be
built were one starting from scratch, harks back to classical ideas about the life men enjoyed in the Golden Age,
before work, money or law were known (as described
in Ovid's *Metamorphoses*, Book I). There is a specific
source for many of its details in Montaigne's essay 'Of

the Cannibals'. This includes an account of the customs used by the native American races, whom European explorers were now encountering for the first time (quoted here in John Florio's English translation, 1603):

It is a nation ... that hath no kind of traffic, no knowledge of letters, no intelligence of numbers, no name of magistrate, nor of politic superiority; no use of service, of riches or of poverty; no contracts, no successions, no partitions, no occupation but idle; no respect of kindred, but common, no apparel but natural, no manuring of lands, no use of wine, corn, or metal. The very words that import lying, falsehood, treason, dissimulations, covetousness, envy, detraction, and pardon, were never heard of amongst them.

See the discussion in the Introduction, pp. lv–lvii.

147 *by contraries*: In opposition to normal practice.
148 *traffic*: Trade.
150 *Letters*: Learning.
151 *service*: Servants.
    succession: Inheritance.
152 *Bourn, bound of land*: Both terms mean 'boundary' (i.e. there would be no private ownership of land).
    tilth: Agriculture.
154 *occupation*: Employment.
156 *Yet he would be king on't*: Antonio points out that this last condition contradicts 145.
159 *in common*: For communal use.
161 *engine*: Machine; here, particularly, weapon.
163 *Of it own kind*: By its own nature.
    foison: Plenty.
166 *idle*: Antonio harks back to Gonzalo's word at 154 and brings out its pejorative implications in contemporary social thought. Idleness might look attractive in the Golden Age, but in 1611 it was regarded as a social threat, and connoted unruliness, criminality and sexual looseness.
170 *nothing*: Perhaps this echoes the Greek word *utopia*, which literally means 'no-place'.

172 *minister occasion*: Provide opportunity (for wit).

173 *sensible*: Sensitive, acute.

179 *An*: If.

    flat-long: With the flat side of the sword, hence ineffective.

180–82 *You would lift the moon . . . without changing*: Gonzalo
    mocks the lords' arrogance: they would change the
    course of the moon, if she would stay still long enough
    for them to do it.

181 *sphere*: Orbit.

183 *a-bat-fowling*: Catching birds at night, when they are
    roosting, by hitting them with sticks (bats): Antonio
    would use the moon as his lantern.

185–6 *adventure my discretion so weakly*: Risk my good judge-
    ment (by becoming angry) on such feeble grounds (as
    you give me).

187 *heavy*: Drowsy.

192 *omit*: Disregard.

    the heavy offer of it: I.e. the chance of sleep.

202 *as by consent*: As if they had agreed to do so.

206 *Th'occasion speaks thee*: The opportunity calls out to
    you.

208 *waking*: Awake.

210 *sleepy*: Dreamlike.

215 *wink'st*: Keep your eyes closed (to opportunity).

219 *if heed me*: If you heed me.

220 *Trebles thee o'er*: Makes you three times greater than
    you are now.

    standing water: Neither ebbing nor flowing (i.e. open
    to persuasion either way).

222 *Hereditary sloth*: (1) Natural laziness; (2) the idleness
    imposed on me by my inherited situation as a younger
    brother.

223–5 *If you but knew . . . invest it*: Antonio tells Sebastian that
    his self-deprecating remarks conceal his real desires
    from himself: although he pretends to mock ambition,
    he secretly nurtures it.

225 *invest*: Clothe.

    Ebbing men: Men who are in decline.

228 *setting*: Fixed look.

229 *A matter*: Something of importance.

230 *throes thee much to yield*: Costs you much pain to bring forth.

231–3 *Although this lord of weak remembrance ... earthed*: Antonio begins by insulting Gonzalo's poor memory – perhaps referring to the confusion over Tunis and Carthage – then shifts to how quickly Gonzalo himself will be forgotten after his death.

234 *spirit*: Quintessence.

234–5 *only | Professes to persuade*: Giving advice is all he ever tries to do.

239 *that way*: In relation to Ferdinand's safety.

241–2 *Ambition cannot pierce ... discovery there*: Antonio's general sense is that the prospect of achieving the crown is so inspiring that ambition itself could imagine nothing higher, and doubts the possibility of anything beyond (or maybe doubts the reality of it). The passage is very opaque and no explanation is wholly satisfactory. It could be corrupt, but perhaps Antonio is avoiding saying exactly what he means. The obscurity of his language corresponds to the darkness of his suggestions.

246 *Ten leagues beyond man's life*: Thirty miles further than anyone could travel in his lifetime. Antonio exaggerates Claribel's remoteness, but the point is not that she really is impossibly distant, but that her exotic marriage has destroyed her political value, by removing her from Europe and making it unlikely that she will ever inherit Naples (a consideration that Sebastian immediately raises, 255–7). In terms of miles, Tunis is closer to Naples than Milan is, but the real gulf between them is cultural and political.

246–9 *she that from Naples ... rough and razorable*: Unless the messenger travelled as fast as the sun, news from Naples would take as long to reach Tunis as for babies to grow to adulthood.

249 *that from whom*: In coming from whom.

250 *cast*: Vomited up (continuing the metaphor of *sea-swallowed*).

251 *that destiny*: As Prospero's brother, Antonio thinks in the same terms. He too sees this as a moment of destiny.

252 *what's past*: What's happened so far.

253 *In yours and my discharge*: For the two of us to execute.

257 *cubit*: About twenty inches.

259 *Measure us*: Retrace, traverse (as if spoken by the cubits).

265–6 *make | A chough of as deep chat*: Train a jackdaw to speak as wisely as Gonzalo, or perhaps, could be myself as much of a jackdaw as Gonzalo is.

266–7 *bore | The mind that I do*: Thought the same way as me, or perhaps, were as resolute as I am.

269 *content*: Contentment.

270 *Tender*: Regard.

273 *feater*: With a better fit.

276–8 *If 'twere a kibe ... in my bosom*: If my conscience hurt me physically, like a chilblain (*kibe*), I would relieve it somehow; but I feel no inner proddings.

279 *candied be they*: Let them be turned into sugar.

280 *molest*: Cause inconvenience.

283 *steel*: Dagger.

285 *perpetual wink*: Everlasting sleep.

286 *morsel*: Piece of meat.

287 *upbraid our course*: Criticize our actions (because he'll be dead).

289 *tell the clock to*: Agree with (whatever our judgement of the right time is).

296 *with music*: F adds *and song*, presumably an elaboration by the copyist, since Ariel does not actually enter singing.

297–9 *My master through his art ... keep them living*: Ariel speaks to Gonzalo, but is heard only by the audience.

299 *project*: Plan (at this time particularly used of an alchemical experiment).

309 *ghastly*: Fearful.

321 *verily*: True.

II.2

In contrast to the powerful aristocrats of II.1, the survivors that Caliban encounters are low-status servants: a jester (a professional

fool, who wears motley: see III.2.63) and a butler. Caliban's
amazement at what he takes for their sophistication and his faith
that they will rescue him from slavery to Prospero are sadly
misplaced. Trinculo and Stephano's vulgarity is signalled in their
language, as they both speak ordinary prose. However, Caliban's
speech hovers on the hinterland between prose and verse. When
he is not actually speaking verse, his lines often contain ghostly
pentameters and are sometimes arranged by editors as blank verse.
This helps to suggest that although Caliban is taken in by Stephano
and Trinculo, he has a sensitivity that sets him apart from them.

  2 *flats*: Swamps.
  3 *inch-meal*: Inch by inch.
  4 *nor*: Neither.
  5 *urchin-shows*: Apparitions, perhaps in the form of
    hedgehogs.
  6 *firebrand*: Will-o'-the-wisp.
  9 *Sometime like*: Sometimes they appear like.
    mow: Grimace.
  13 *wound with*: Entwined by.
  17 *mind*: Notice.
  18 *bear off*: Ward off.
  21 *bombard*: Leather jug.
  27 *poor-John*: Dried, salted hake (a poor man's food).
  29 *painted*: Painted on a sign. Trinculo imagines himself
    taking this dead *monster* back to England and exhibiting
    him in a fairground booth, alongside all the other freaks
    displayed there for money.
  30 *make a man*: (1) Make a man's fortune; (2) be equal to
    a man.
  32 *doit*: Half a farthing; a very small coin.
  33 *dead Indian*: A series of native Americans were brought
    back to England by explorers in the early seventeenth
    century, as curiosities. Usually they quickly succumbed
    to disease or to the climate.
  34–5 *let loose my opinion*: Change my mind (since Caliban
    has legs and is warm-blooded, he can't be a fish).
  38 *gaberdine*: Long, loose cloak; Caliban's simple garment.
  39–40 *Misery acquaints a man with strange bedfellows*: A
    proverb that is absurdly appropriate for this situation.

44 *scurvy*: Worthless.

46 *swabber*: Sailor who washes the decks (the lowliest of ranks).

50 *tang*: Stinging effect.

52 *tar . . . pitch*: Substances used in ship-building.

53 *tailor*: Tailors were proverbially lecherous, as their occupation allowed them intimate access to women.

56 *Do not torment me*: Caliban reacts to Trinculo's trembling (see 80), which he takes as the beginning of another spirit torture such as those described in 4–14.

58 *men of Ind*: Indian natives (the phrase appears in the Coverdale and Bishops' Bibles as a synonym for 'black moor').

61 *on four legs*: The normal idiom is 'as proper a man as ever went on two legs'. Caliban and Trinculo both have their heads under the cloak; Stephano takes the object for a monster with four legs and no head.

63 *at'*: At his. The usual abbreviation would be 'at's nostrils', but the resulting clash of sounds has led to the 's' being suppressed.

66 *an ague*: Caliban is shivering with fear; or perhaps it is Trinculo (see 80).

68–70 *If I can recover him . . . on neat's leather*: Like Trinculo, Stephano's first reaction to Caliban is to wonder how he can make money out of him. His notion is that Caliban could be given as a present to some ruler, who would then reward Stephano with cash or a pension.

70 *neat's leather*: Cowhide.

73–4 *after the wisest*: In the wisest fashion.

75 *go near*: Do much.

76–7 *I will not take too much for him*: I.e. no price will be too high for him; it is impossible for me to sell him too dear.

83 *cat*: Echoing the proverb, 'Ale will make a cat speak'.

87 *chops*: Jaws.

90 *delicate*: Delightful; cf. I.2.272, where Prospero praises Ariel with the same adjective.

93 *detract*: Speak disparagingly.

98–9 *I have no long spoon*: Another proverb: 'He must have a long spoon that will sup with the devil.'

106 *siege*: Excrement.

106–7 *mooncalf*: Monster (since idiots or misshapen births were supposed to be caused by the influence of the moon).

107 *vent*: Excrete.

116 *an if*: If.

    sprites: Spirits.

121 *butt of sack*: Cask of white wine.

130 *kiss the book*: Stephano offers Trinculo another drink, but the phrase refers to the Bible, which would be kissed to confirm an oath.

131 *goose*: Simpleton.

138 *when time was*: Once upon a time. This is the kind of claim made by explorers to take advantage of the willingness of natives to believe that gods took human shape.

139–40 *My mistress*: Miranda.

140 *thy dog, and thy bush*: These were the customary attributes of the man in the moon who, according to folk belief, was banished to the moon for gathering brushwood on a Sunday. They reappear in *A Midsummer Night's Dream*, when Starveling dresses up in the role of Moonshine (V.1.250–52).

144 *By this good light*: By the sun.

147 *drawn*: Drunk.

148 *I'll show thee every fertile inch o'th'island*: The welcome and trust that Caliban gives to Stephano exactly repeat his experiences twelve years earlier with Prospero (I.2.336–8).

151 *When's*: When his.

    rob: Steal.

154–5 *puppy-headed*: Stupid.

159 *abominable*: Spelled *abhominable* in F, as was customary at this time, on the assumption that it was equivalent to the Latin *ab homine*, 'inhuman or beastly'.

167 *crabs*: Crab-apples.

168 *pignuts*: An edible tuber, that has to be dug up, not pulled.

169 *a jay's nest*: For its eggs.

170 *marmoset*: Described as good for food by early explorers.

171 *filberts*: Hazelnuts.

172 *scamels*: This is not recorded as a word anywhere else: the sense appears to be some kind of shellfish or rock-pool creature. Probably this is a textual misreading by the printer or the copyist. Some editors have suggested emending to 'sea-mels' or 'sea-mews', i.e. gulls; to 'squamelle', a French word meaning 'scaly'; or to 'stannels', another name for the kestrel. But these are all guesses, and no wholly satisfactory alternative has so far been found.

175 *inherit*: Succeed; take over.

180 *dams*: Used to create pools in rivers, in order to catch fish.

181 *firing*: Firewood.

182 *trencher*: Wooden plate.

184 *get a new man*: Addressed to Prospero.

185 *high-day*: Day of celebration, holiday. There is, of course, a profound contradiction between *Freedom, high-day* and *Ca-Caliban | Has a new master*. Caliban is the rebellious slave who imagines himself to have achieved his freedom. In fact, he has merely exchanged one master for a worse.

III.1

Ferdinand's log-carrying gives a chivalric cast to his devotion to Miranda. Like a knight of romance, he proves his love by enduring a test (see 65–7). But it also harks back to Prospero's words about making his courtship *uneasy . . . lest too light winning | Make the prize light* (I.2.451–2). Ferdinand has to earn Miranda's hand by hard labour, and will be taught by this to value her all the more.

1–2 *There be some sports . . . in them sets off*: Some recreations involve physical discomfort, but the pleasure they bring compensates for the effort.

2 *baseness*: Menial activity. Ferdinand is anxious that manual labour will compromise his status as a gentleman, but reassures himself that it is redeemed by the cause in which it is endured.

4 *ends*: Results.
   mean: Humble.

5 *heavy*: Wearisome.

6 *quickens*: Brings to life.

8 *crabbed*: Sour.

11 *sore injunction*: Stern command.

12-13 *such baseness | Had never like executor*: Such a lowly task was never performed by someone so noble.

13 *I forget*: Ferdinand resumes his work, which he had halted while talking to the audience.

15 *Most busy, least when I do it*: Ferdinand comments that *sweet thoughts* like these make his labours endurable, and that they are most active in his mind when he rests for a moment (as he does during this speech). Some editors emend *busie lest* in F to 'busilest', explaining it as a contracted form of the rare adverb 'busiliest' (= most busy). This gives the meaning 'such comforting thoughts come most upon me while I labour'.
   Prospero following at a distance: The presence of Prospero in this scene underlines that the developing relationship between Miranda and Ferdinand is part of his plan for returning to Italy. He cannot make her fall in love with Ferdinand, but he needs it to happen in order to create the new alliance that he wants between Naples and Milan. See Introduction, pp. xxxix–xlii.

19 *'Twill weep*: The log will exude resin when it burns; Miranda imagines this, poetically, as its tears.

31 *worm*: Creature.
   thou art infected: You've caught the plague of love. As at the more famous moment when Miranda meets the rest of the Europeans (V.1.181–4), there is a strong tension between her innocent enthusiasm and her father's disenchantment. Prospero expects the illusions of love will not last; he is more focused on the political benefits that can be made from them.

32 *visitation*: (1) Visit to Ferdinand; (2) outbreak of symptoms.

34 *by at night*: Nearby at night-time (a conventional

expression of love: Ferdinand has not yet spent an
evening on the island).

37 *hest*: Command.

38 *top of admiration*: Epitome of wonder.

42 *diligent*: Attentive.
    several: Various.

45 *owed*: Owned.

46 *put it to the foil*: Thwart it, defeat it (a metaphor from
    fencing, developing the idea of a woman's defect 'quar-
    relling' with her graces).

47-8 *created | Of every creature's best*: Made by combining
    the best parts of every creature.

50 *glass*: Looking-glass.

50-52 *Nor have I seen ... my dear father*: Evidently Miranda
    has changed her mind about Caliban, whom she counted
    as a man at I.2.444-5.

52 *How features are abroad*: What people look like else-
    where.

53 *skilless*: Ignorant.
    modesty: Virginity.

54 *dower*: Dowry.

56 *form*: Devise.

58 *my father's precepts*: Presumably Prospero has instilled
    the idea into Miranda that excess speech is a female
    vice.

59 *condition*: Rank.

61 *would not*: Wish it were not.

62-3 *suffer | The flesh-fly blow my mouth*: Allow the carrion-
    fly to lay its eggs in my mouth.

66 *to it*: To your service.

69 *kind event*: Happy outcome.

70-71 *if hollowly ... to mischief*: If I speak insincerely, turn
    the best fortune that is promised (*boded*) me into bad.

79 *die to want*: Die for lack of. Miranda is offering herself
    to Ferdinand, and although her words primarily refer
    to her affections, they also offer a delicate testimony to
    her awakening sexual desire. This implication continues
    into her next remark about the impossibility of hiding
    her desire – with its underlying metaphor of pregnancy

– and to her self-rebuke, *bashful cunning* (81), which
admits that her modest phrases conceal more robust
meanings.

84 *maid*: (1) Servant; (2) virgin.

88–9 *as willing | As bondage e'er of freedom*: As eager (to
enter your service) as ever a slave (*bondage*) longed for
freedom.

93 *withal*: Therewith.

96 *appertaining*: Related to this.

III.2

In this scene, Trinculo stands slightly apart from the conversa-
tion taking place between Stephano and Caliban. This allows
Ariel to throw his voice in his direction, making it appear that
Trinculo is interrupting and contradicting their plotting.

1 *Tell not me*: Stephano is in the middle of a conversation; probably Trinculo has told him to be more sparing
of the wine.
out: Empty.

2–3 *bear up, and board 'em*: Approach and attack (a phrase
from sea-warfare, but used here of the bottle).

6 *brained*: I.e. drunk.

8–9 *Thy eyes are almost set in thy head*: A slang expression
meaning 'you're drunk'. In the next line, Trinculo
pretends to take the remark literally.

14 *five and thirty leagues*: About a hundred miles.

16 *standard*: Ensign, standard-bearer.

17 *he's no standard*: I.e. he's too drunk to stand upright.

18 *run*: Run away (from battle).

19 *go*: Walk.
lie: (1) Lie down; (2) tell lies.

25 *in case*: In a fit state.

32 *natural*: Fool.

35 *the next tree*: (You'll be hanged from) the nearest tree.

38 *suit*: Request. This is a parody of life at an Italian court;
Antonio, as Prospero recollected, quickly learnt how
to *grant suits* (I.2.79).

48 *in's*: In his.

49 *supplant*: Remove (usually used in a political sense, as
at II.1.271, III.3.70).

51 *Mum*: Be quiet.

55 *this thing*: Trinculo.

58 *compassed*: Contrived.

61 *knock a nail into his head*: In the Bible (Judges 4:21), this is the manner in which Sisera was killed by Jael.

63 *pied ninny*: Parti-coloured simpleton. Trinculo wears 'motley', the professional costume of a jester.
patch: Fool (from the name of the jester who served Cardinal Wolsey).

67 *quick freshes*: Running streams of fresh water.

70 *stockfish*: Dried cod (which had to be beaten before it could be cooked).

80 *murrain*: Plague.

80–81 *devil take your fingers*: Trinculo curses Stephano's hand for striking him.

91 *paunch him*: Stab him in the belly.

92 *weasand*: Windpipe.

94 *sot*: Fool.

96 *rootedly*: Groundedly, firmly.

97 *utensils*: Household furnishings. Caliban tells Stephano to destroy only the magic books, leaving Prospero's goods as plunder.

98 *deck*: Furnish.

101 *nonpareil*: Paragon; someone without equal.

102 *she*: Her.

104 *brave*: Fine.

105 *become*: Adorn.

111 *Excellent*: Presumably Trinculo sounds less than enthusiastic, prompting Stephano to make things up with him.

118 *jocund*: Merry.
troll the catch: Sing the song. A 'catch' is a short song (often a drinking song) sung as a round. Cf. *Twelfth Night*, II.3.58–72.

119 *but whilere*: Just a little while ago.

122 *Flout 'em and scout 'em*: Mock them and jeer at them.

124 *Thought is free*: A proverb, meaning 'however controlled our bodies are, inwardly we can think whatever we like'. But on Prospero's island there are many

ways in which thought is subject to hidden manipula-
tion.

125 *tabor*: Small drum.

127–8 *the picture of Nobody*: A figure of a man, with head,
legs and arms but no body, appeared on the 1606 title
page of the anonymous comedy *Nobody and Somebody*.
Its publisher, John Trundle (who also issued the first
quarto of *Hamlet*, 1603), had the sign of Nobody
outside his shop.

130 *as thou list*: As you please.

132 *He that dies pays all debts*: A proverb expressing
bravado, but Stephano's courage does not hold out.

136 *noises*: (1) Sounds; (2) consorts of music.

138 *twangling instruments*: Plucked stringed instruments
seem to be implied, such as lutes.

142 *The clouds methought would open*: Caliban's meaning is
self-evident, but his image is also reminiscent of the
Jacobean court masques, with their spectacular scenic
effects, usually performed to the accompaniment of rich
music.

148 *by and by*: Shortly.

152 *lays it on*: Drums enthusiastically.

153 *Wilt come*: Probably spoken to Caliban.

III.3

The action of this scene alludes to an episode in Virgil's *Aeneid*.
In Book III, Aeneas and his companions, wandering the
Mediterranean in search of a site for their new capital, arrive at
the Strophades islands. There their attempts to dine are prevented
by a flock of harpies that swoop down on their food and befoul
it. The harpies prophesy that Aeneas must make his way to Italy,
but warn that he will suffer famine before reaching there, as a
punishment for having attacked them.

1 *By'r lakin*: By our Ladykin (the Virgin Mary).

3 *forthrights and meanders*: Straight paths and winding
paths (as in a maze).

5 *attached*: Seized.

8 *for my flatterer*: As if it were my flatterer. Alonso imagines his *hope* to be a court sycophant, feeding him with
false expectations.

10 *frustrate*: (1) Defeated; (2) vain.

12 *for one repulse*: Because we were defeated once.

14 *throughly*: Thoroughly.

15 *travail*: (1) Journeying; (2) labour.

17 *Solemn and strange music*: In the Elizabethan theatre, 'solemn' music generally meant wind instruments, such as recorders or cornets; *strange* probably indicates unusual rhythms or melodies.

on the top: A very rare direction, that appears in only one other place in Shakespeare (*Henry VI, Part I*, III.2.25). Probably it refers to the musicians' gallery over the stage. Some editors think that at the Globe Prospero stood in the 'hut' at the very top of the building, from which a trumpet was sounded to signal the start of the play. But this space was not visible from the stage, and Prospero would have been hidden from many of the spectators. At the Blackfriars, the highest point was in the gallery.

20 *kind keepers*: Guardian angels.

21 *living drollery*: Puppet-show, but with living creatures in place of puppets.

23 *phoenix*: A mythical Arabian bird, only one of which existed at any one moment. In time, each phoenix would immolate itself and a new one would spring from its ashes.

25 *want credit*: Lack credibility.

26 *Travellers ne'er did lie*: Antonio means that, having seen these *Shapes*, he will no longer doubt any far-fetched story.

30 *certes*: Certainly.

33 *generation*: Species.

36 *muse*: Wonder at.

39 *Praise in departing*: Save your praise until the end (Prospero knows what is about to follow).

41 *viands*: Food.

stomachs: Appetites.

44 *mountaineers*: Mountain-dwelling people.

46 *Wallets of flesh*: Wattles, folds of skin.

46–7 *men | Whose heads stood in their breasts*: More travellers' tales: it was a widespread belief, deriving ultimately from the Greek geographer Pliny, that some far-off races of men had heads growing below their shoulders. Such stories are told by Othello (*Othello*, I.3.144–5).

48 *Each putter-out of five for one*: English travellers sometimes insured their trips by leaving sums with brokers at home, to be paid back five-fold if they returned safely and with proof that they had reached their destination.

49 *stand to*: Set to work.

52 *harpy*: A mythical creature with a woman's head and breasts, talons for hands and the body and wings of a bird. Harpies were associated with divine retribution. Since Ariel wears wings, it seems likely that in Shakespeare's theatre he was flown in from above (a flying mechanism is used for Juno in IV.1).

  quaint device: Ingenious mechanism (perhaps a reversible table top?).

54–5 *That hath to instrument ... what is in't*: Destiny uses the sublunary world as its instrument through which its purposes are worked out. Ariel's speech, with its demanding and convoluted syntax, is in the style of Prospero, who has scripted it (see 85).

55–6 *the never-surfeited sea | Hath caused to belch up you*: Destiny has caused the always-hungry sea to belch you up.

59 *suchlike valour*: I.e. insane bravery, desperation.

60 *proper*: Own.

61 *elements*: Raw materials.

62 *tempered*: Hardened.

64 *still-closing waters*: Waters that flow together again as soon as they are separated (by attempts to 'stab' them).

65 *One dowl*: Even the smallest feather.

66 *like*: Similarly.

67 *massy*: Heavy.

71 *requit*: Repaid (they are punished by the sea, as they used the sea to try to kill Prospero and Miranda).

73 *powers*: Deities.

74 *all the creatures*: All creation.

75 *peace*: Peace of conscience.

77 *Ling'ring perdition*: Gradual ruin, slow destruction.

77–8 *any death . . . at once*: Any single or sudden death.

78 *attend*: Wait upon.

79 *whose wraths*: This refers back to the *powers* of 73. Ariel warns the courtiers that the only way of escaping divine anger is to repent and live blameless future lives. There is no other protection for them in this empty island.

82 *mocks and mows*: Mocking grimaces.

84 *a grace it had, devouring*: I.e. you looked graceful even while you caused the food to be devoured or removed. Harpies were normally represented as vile creatures.

85 *bated*: Left out.

86 *so*: Similarly.

86–7 *good life | And observation strange*: Great spirit and precise imitativeness.

88 *several kinds*: Individual parts.

90 *distractions*: Mental disturbances.

91 *fits*: Transports of mind.

94–5 *I'th'name of something holy . . . strange stare*: Evidently Ariel's speech was audible only to the *three men of sin*.

99 *bass my trespass*: Proclaim my sin in a bass voice, or provide a musical ground, or *bass*, for my guilt.

101 *plummet*: Plumb-line (a lead weight on a cord used by sailors to test the depth of water).

103 *their legions o'er*: All the devils of hell (if they come one by one).

105 *given to work a great time after*: Delayed a long time in its action.

107 *of suppler joints*: Fitter than me.

108 *ecstasy*: Frenzy.

IV.1

The masque performed for Ferdinand and Miranda in this scene is a theatrical celebration of a kind that was customary at great festival occasions in princely courts all over seventeenth-century Europe. The lovers are presented with a little drama, a series of songs and some formal dances; in masques at the English court, such devices would have been followed with general dances, or *revels* (see 148), in which the performers invited spectators to join them on the floor.

Such masques were often staged to mark great court marriages. Ferdinand and Miranda are merely at the point of betrothal – hence Prospero's remarkable insistence on the need to avoid sexual relations until the formal marriage rites have taken place (14–22, 51–4; see Introduction, pp. xliii–xlv). Nonetheless, his masque effectively cements the personal and political union between his daughter and Alonso's son (the *contract* of 84 and 133).

1 *austerely*: Severely.

3 *a third of mine own life*: Probably Prospero simply means 'a significant part'. Editors have worried that some more specific reference may be implied, as for example a distinction between his daughter, dukedom and art. But the phrase makes sense as it stands, and there is a parallel formula at V.1.312.

5 *tender*: Offer.

7 *strangely*: Wonderfully.

8 *this my rich gift*: It is notable that the wedding of Miranda and Ferdinand is not treated romantically, but as a transaction essentially between Ferdinand and Prospero. Like all seventeenth-century fathers, Prospero tends to regard Miranda as a piece of his property to be disposed of, just as she will be the dynastic cement in relations between Naples and Milan.

9 *boast of her*: Boast about her. F has *boast her of*, a reading which some editors believe is correct, though the error would be easy for a compositor to make. Other editors emend it to 'boast her off'.

11 *halt*: Limp.

12 *Against*: Against the word of.

15 *virgin-knot*: Prospero refers to the knotted girdle that was worn by Roman brides as a symbolic token of their chastity; metaphorically he means Miranda's maidenhead.

16 *sanctimonious*: Sacred.

18 *aspersion*: Blessing; literally, a sprinkling of holy water.

20–21 *bestrew . . . your bed with weeds*: In literary celebrations of marriage, the marital bed is often depicted as strewn with flowers.

23 *Hymen's lamps*: Hymen, the Roman god of marriage,

was usually depicted as carrying a bright torch, the symbol of his goodwill towards the married couple.

24 *issue*: Children.

25 *murkiest den*: Darkest hiding place.

26 *opportune*: Convenient (accented on the second syllable).

27 *Our worser genius can*: (That) one's bad angel can make.

29 *edge*: Keen delight.

30–31 *or . . . Or*: Either . . . or.

30 *Phoebus' steeds*: The horses that pull the chariot of Phoebus, the sun-god, here imagined as having gone lame (*foundered*). Ferdinand looks forward to the public celebrations for his marriage, and the keenness with which the newly married couple will long for the marriage bed. It will seem that the day will never be gone, or that night will never rise.

35 *your last service*: The trick played on Alonso in III.3.

37 *rabble*: Crowd (of inferior spirits).

39 *quick*: Lively.

41 *vanity*: Show; illusion.

42 *Presently*: Immediately.

43 *twink*: Winking of an eye.

50 *conceive*: Understand.

51 *true*: True to your word. Prospero returns to the admonitions against premarital sex begun at 14–22.

52 *Too much the rein*: Too much freedom (like a horse let loose).

   straw: Tinder, kindling.

54 *good night*: Farewell to.

56 *the ardour of my liver*: Like the *blood* (53), the liver was believed in Elizabethan physiology to be a reservoir of sexual passion. Ferdinand assures Prospero that he can keep his appetites in check.

57–8 *Bring a corollary, | Rather than want a spirit*: Bring too many spirits, if need be, rather than too few.

58 *pertly*: Promptly.

59 *No tongue*: Be silent. Silence was thought to be necessary during magical operations; cf. 126–7.

   Iris: The rainbow in classical mythology, and one of

the messengers between the heavens and the earth. In this fiction, she has been sent down by Juno (see 70–71).

60 *Ceres*: Goddess of the earth and harvest; her role is played by Ariel (see 167). This speech begins by listing a series of rural qualities associated with Ceres, with no main verb. The action of the sentence is delayed until 72: '[Juno] *Bids thee leave these*'.
leas: Meadows.

61 *vetches*: A coarse crop used as animal feed.

63 *thatched with stover*: Covered like thatch with grass (used as winter fodder for sheep: hence *them to keep*).

64 *peonied*: Covered with flowers (peonies). F has *pioned* and some editors take this to mean 'trenched' or 'excavated' ('pion' is an obsolete verb meaning 'to do the work of a pioneer'), explaining that (with *twillèd*) it refers to tasks performed by labourers in the maintaining ditches, or perhaps to the effects of natural erosion on river-banks and streams. But flowers seem to be meant: they are put there by *April* (65) and used to trim the coronets of the naiads.
twillèd: Woven, plaited.

65 *spongy*: Damp, rainy.

66 *nymphs*: In classical mythology, nymphs are often associated with rivers. Their *coldness* signals their virginity, as do the *crowns* of flowers that April makes for them. But as goddess of childbirth, Juno is a patron of sexuality and approves the productivity of harvest.
broom-groves: Groves of broom (a yellow flowering bush).

67 *dismissèd bachelor*: Rejected lover.

68 *pole-clipped*: Probably this means that the vines are twined around their supporting poles, as if embracing them, though some editors interpret it as 'poll-clipped', that is pollarded, pruned.

69 *sea-marge*: Seashore.

70 *queen o'th'sky*: Juno, queen of the gods, and goddess of childbirth. She was associated with the air; the masque thus presents a transaction between the air and the earth (= Ceres).

71 *watery arch*: Rainbow.

72 *Juno descends*: The goddess arrives in a flying machine
   that lowers her from the 'heavens' over the stage to the
   floor. However, twenty-five lines elapse before she joins
   the conversation and some editors conjecture that the
   stage direction has been inserted in the text too early
   and should appear at 101. If the direction is correct, it
   suggests that Juno hovers over the stage during the
   dialogue, as the presiding deity whom the other two
   wait to greet. A third possibility is that no flying
   machine is involved and that Juno simply manifests
   herself in the gallery over the stage, then descends
   behind to emerge at stage level: *I know her by her gait*
   (102) could imply an entrance by walking. It is impossible to be certain about the stagecraft involved, and
   probably Shakespeare expected the actors would adapt
   the dialogue to whatever scenic resources they had to
   hand.

74 *peacocks*: Sacred to Juno; here they pull her chariot
   through the sky.
   amain: Swiftly.

75 *entertain*: Welcome.

78 *saffron*: Yellow-coloured.

81 *bosky*: Wooded.
   unshrubbed down: Treeless downlands (the arch of the
   rainbow rests on these two contrasting spots).

83 *short-grassed green*: In court masques, the dancing
   generally took place on a floor covered with a baize
   cloth (cf. 130).

85 *donation*: Gift.
   estate: Bestow.

87 *Venus or her son*: The goddess of love, and Cupid
   (often represented as *blind* (90), i.e. blindfolded), are
   here invoked as symbols of unruly lust or merely
   physical desire. As Iris explains (94–101), they had
   hoped to manifest their power by arousing lustful
   appetites in Ferdinand and Miranda, but are symbolically excluded from this celebration. It is central to
   Prospero's masque that, although it praises marital

union (Juno) and fertility (Ceres), it dwells on the
need to restrain desire and keep love within the boundaries of marriage.

89 *dusky*: Dark.

   Dis: One of the Latin names of Pluto, ruler of the
   underworld. In the well-known myth told in Ovid's
   Metamorphoses, Book V, Proserpine, daughter of Ceres,
   is abducted by Dis, and henceforth spends half the year
   in the underworld. This was commonly understood as
   an allegory of the seasonal change between winter and
   summer. Cf. *The Winter's Tale*, IV.4.116–18.

90 *scandalled*: Disgraced, shameful.

93 *Paphos*: In Cyprus, home of the goddess and her cult.

94 *Dove-drawn*: Doves were sacred to Venus, as peacocks
   were to Juno, and drew her chariot.

96 *bed-right*: Consummation of the marriage. A Shakespearean coinage: intercourse between husband and
   wife is imagined as a monetary debt which has to be
   paid.

98 *Mars's hot minion*: In classical mythology, Venus, the
   wife of Vulcan, had an adulterous affair with Mars.
   is returned again: Has gone home.

99 *waspish-headed*: Peevish, given to stinging.

100 *sparrows*: Regarded as lecherous.

101 *a boy right out*: An ordinary boy.

102 *gait*: Bearing. In Virgil's *Aeneid*, I.404–5, Aeneas recog-
    nizes his mother, Venus, by her footstep.

106 *Honour, riches, marriage-blessing*: Juno was goddess of
    wealth and honour, as well as patroness of marriage.

110 *foison*: Abundance.

111 *garners*: Granaries.

114–15 *Spring come to you . . . end of harvest*: May your harvest-
    time be immediately followed by a new spring, without
    any intervening winter.

121 *confines*: Natural elements.

122 *My present fancies*: The ideas in my mind (the masque
    is an illusion created by the spirits to mirror Prospero's
    thoughts).

123 *So rare a wondered father and a wife*: Editors disagree

over whether Shakespeare wrote 'and a wife' (referring to Miranda) or 'and a wise' (referring to Prospero,
in a grammatical idiom that sounds odd to modern ears
but appears elsewhere in Shakespeare). The spelling of
'wife/wise' looks different in different copies of F,
making it very hard to say whether the printer used an
'f' or a long 's' (∫). Some editors believe it was an 'f'
that broke and lost its cross-piece during the printing;
others argue that the cross-piece which seems to be
there in some copies is really just a blot. In fact, the
compositor might have set up either an 'f' or an '∫',
since in early modern printing the two letters were
prone to drift into the wrong boxes (what today we
call a 'foulcase error'), and if magnification could
demonstrate for certain which letter was used, there
would still be arguments for emending in either direction. In effect, the true reading is undecidable, and
whichever version we print is ultimately a matter of
subjective editorial preference.

128 *naiads*: Water-nymphs.
windring: Winding and wandering (this word does not
appear anywhere else in Shakespeare, or in any other
author).

129 *sedged crowns*: Coronets woven from sedge (a riverside
plant).

130 *crisp*: Rippling.

132 *temperate*: Modest, chaste (in contrast to the *sunburned*
reapers).

134 *of August weary*: Because reapers work hard during the
harvest.

138 *country footing*: Rustic dance.
properly habited: Suitably dressed.
heavily: Sorrowfully.

142 *Avoid*: Begone.

144 *works him strongly*: Upsets him greatly.

145 *distempered*: Out of temper.

146 *moved sort*: Disturbed state.

149 *As I foretold you*: See 120–22.

150 *into thin air*: Spirits were thought to become visible

through a thickening of the airy element of which they were composed. By returning to *thin air* they would disappear from sight. Cf. V.1.21, where Prospero calls Ariel *thou, which art but air*, and John Donne's poem 'Air and Angels'.

151 *fabric*: Structure, creation. It is *baseless* because, being an illusion, it lacks substance: cf. the *insubstantial pageant* (155).

153 *the great globe*: Prospero means 'the whole world', but he also puns on the name of Shakespeare's playhouse, the Globe. The other buildings listed at 152–3 further bring to mind the spectacular illusionist effects of masques at court, which often depicted opulent architectural settings. Their marvellous changing machinery (not yet in use at the public theatres) made it appear that scenes 'dissolved' into one another magically; or Prospero may be alluding to the contrast between their illusory scenic splendours and the dull world, untouched by illusion, to which spectators returned after the event.

154 *all which it inherit*: All people who will subsequently occupy it; cf. Matthew 5:5: 'The meek shall inherit the earth'.

156 *rack*: Shred of cloud.
We are such stuff: Prospero shifts from talking about the spirits and their fragile illusions to reflecting on the brief existence that he and fellow human beings have. In 148–56 the masque is a metaphor for life, but 156–8 refers to life itself.

157 *on*: Of.

158 *rounded*: (1) Completed; (2) surrounded (since there is no consciousness of anything before birth or after death).

167 *When I presented Ceres*: Presumably Ariel means he played Ceres' role, though this could simply mean that he produced the masque, or that he played Iris and so *presented* Ceres, i.e. introduced her. But since Iris does not sing, and Ariel's role is designed for an accomplished singer, this seems unlikely.

170 *varlets*: Rogues.

174 *For kissing of their feet*: For simply being under their feet. Ariel means that they were so fired up (*red-hot*, 171) with misplaced energy that they picked fights with the air and the ground; or perhaps he is describing their drunken staggering and heavy tread.

174-5 *bending | Towards*: Pursuing.

176 *unbacked*: Unbroken.

177 *Advanced*: Raised; cf. I.2.408.

178 *As*: As if.

179 *lowing*: Mooing (the men follow the music like a calf following the cow).

182 *filthy-mantled*: Covered with scum (like a mantle or cloak).

184 *O'erstunk*: Smelt worse than.

186 *trumpery*: Showy rubbish.

187 *stale*: Decoy.

189 *Nurture*: Education, good upbringing.

192 *cankers*: Grows rotten.

193 *line*: Lime tree. 'Line' is a variant form of 'lime' or 'linden', and in the early modern period wet clothes were often hung out to dry on bushes. It is possible, though, that Prospero literally means clothes-line, and in practice most modern productions use a line. There is a *line-grove* around Prospero's cell: see V.1.10.

194-5 *that the blind mole may not hear a footfall*: Moles were thought to have exceptionally acute hearing because of their dark life underground.

198 *jack*: Knave, trickster.

205 *prize*: Reward.

206 *hoodwink this mischance*: Cover up this misfortune, make it forgotten (in falconry, birds are kept quiet by being 'hoodwinked' with caps over their heads).

213 *fetch off*: Retrieve.
    o'er ears: Up to the ears (in the pool).

222 *King Stephano! O peer*: This refers to a popular Elizabethan ballad also mentioned in *Othello*, II.3.84-5: 'King Stephen was and-a worthy peer, | His breeches cost him but a crown.'

223 *wardrobe*: Literally, a collection of clothes, but at this time the Wardrobe was also the name of one of the departments of the royal court.

226 *frippery*: Second-hand clothes shop (i.e. these garments are much better than *trash*).

230 *dropsy*: A disease involving water-retention.

231 *luggage*: Useless baggage.

233 *pinches*: Cramps.

235 *Mistress line*: Humorously addressed to the tree.

236 *jerkin*: Short, close-fitting jacket.

under the line: Off the line. Stephano's ensuing jokes pun on the nautical meaning of 'line' as the equator, and the idea that sailors might lose their hair in the southern hemisphere, either from scurvy or from tropical or venereal disease.

238 *by line and level*: According to the rule; literally, the plumb-line and carpenter's level.

an't like: If it please.

242–3 *pass of pate*: Sally of wit.

244 *lime*: Birdlime (a sticky substance used to catch birds, and which would cause clothes to stick to one's fingers).

247 *barnacles*: Shellfish, or perhaps barnacle geese (believed at this time to grow from shellfish dropped into water).

248 *villainous*: Vilely.

249 *lay to your fingers*: Put your fingers to work.

250 *hogshead*: Large barrel.

257 *charge*: Command.

258 *dry convulsions*: Aches produced by an absence of moistness in the body.

259 *agèd cramps*: Cramps such as the elderly have.

pinch-spotted: Bruised by pinches.

260 *pard*: Leopard.

cat-o'-mountain: Wildcat.

V.1

0 *Enter Prospero . . . and Ariel*: Prospero and Ariel enter together, although they had only left the stage moments before. At the Blackfriars playhouse, used by Shakespeare's company as well as the Globe, it was customary to have music between the acts; hence there would have

been a structural pause before the beginning of the next scene. At the Globe, where staging was continuous, some rearrangement of the dialogue might have been necessary, though Prospero perhaps needs to leave the stage in order to reassume his *magic robes*.

1 *gather to a head*: Come to a climax (like *project*, a phrase used in the jargon of alchemy).

2–3 *time | Goes upright with his carriage*: Time is imagined as an old man, now walking without stooping because his burden has become so little.

3 *How's the day*: What time is it?

5 *I did say so*: See I.2.240 and note.

10 *line-grove*: Grove of limes (linden-trees).
    weather-fends: Protects from the weather.

11 *till your release*: Until you release them.

17 *eaves of reeds*: Thatched roofs (down which *winter's drops* run).

18 *affections*: Feelings.

21 *touch*: Apprehension.

23–4 *that relish . . . Passion as they*: Who feels suffering every bit as acutely as they do.

24 *kindlier*: (1) More compassionately; (2) more according to our kind, to human affinities. Prospero affirms that, as a human being, he should not feel the sufferings of other humans less than Ariel, who is merely a spirit.

25 *high wrongs*: Great injuries (to me).

26–7 *with my nobler reason 'gainst my fury | Do I take part*: Prospero imagines the impulses to forgive and to revenge as debating within his psyche. The *nobler* course is to forgive, and suppress the *fury* of his resentments.

27 *rarer*: (1) More unusual; (2) finer.

28 *They being penitent*: If they are sorry. Of course, Prospero's fine sentiments are tripped up by what follows: the reconciliation with Antonio and Sebastian will not seem entirely complete.

33–50 *Ye elves of hills . . . By my so potent art*: This passage draws on a magical incantation that the Roman poet Ovid puts into the mouth of the sorceress Medea, in his *Metamorphoses* (VII.192–209). This is a speech that every Elizabethan schoolboy would have known in the original Latin, though Shakespeare also echoes the 1567 translation by Arthur Golding:

> Ye airs and winds: ye elves of hills, of brooks, of
>   woods alone,
> Of standing lakes, and of the night, approach ye every
>   one.
> Through help of whom (the crooked banks much
>   wondering at the thing)
> I have compelled streams to run clean backward to their
>   spring.
> By charms I make the calm seas rough, and make the
>   rough seas plain,
> And cover all the sky with clouds and chase them
>   thence again.
> By charms I raise and lay the winds, and burst the
>   viper's jaw,
> And from the bowels of the earth both stones and trees
>   do draw.
> Whole woods and forests I remove; I make the moun-
>   tains shake,
> And even the earth itself to groan and fearfully to
>   quake.
> I call up dead men from their graves, and thee, O light-
>   some moon,
> I darken oft, though beaten brass abate thy peril soon.
> Our sorcery dims the morning fair, and darks the sun at
>   noon.

33 *standing*: Not flowing.

36 *demi-puppets*: Fairies of half-sized or puppet-like appearance.

37 *green sour ringlets*: Fairy rings in the grass.

39 *midnight mushrooms*: Mushrooms that spring up overnight.

40 *curfew*: Evening bell (after which the spirits are free to roam until sunrise; cf. I.2.327).

41 *masters*: Ministers, rulers within their domains (cf. I.2.275).

43 *azured vault*: Blue sky.

45 *fire*: I.e. lightning.

    rifted: Split.

    Jove's stout oak: The oak tree was sacred to Jove.

46 *his own bolt*: Jove was god of thunder.

47 *spurs*: Roots.

50 *rough*: (1) Violent; (2) crude.

51 *abjure*: Renounce.

53 *their senses that*: The senses of those whom.

54 *This airy charm*: Prospero means the *heavenly music*, which will help cure the court party's mental distraction. In Neoplatonic thought, music was thought to mirror the harmonies of the universe, and hence to have harmonizing power on the mind. Cf. 58–60.

57 *which Prospero observing, speaks*: Prospero, having observed this, speaks.

58–60 *A solemn air . . . thy skull*: Probably Prospero speaks to Alonso, then turns to Gonzalo and the other members of the group. None of this speech is heard by the people to whom it is addressed, as they are still recovering from the spell. They are unaware of Prospero's presence until 106.

59 *unsettled fancy*: Troubled imagination.

63 *sociable*: Humanly sympathetic.

64 *fellowly*: Companionable (i.e. my eyes weep in sympathy with yours).

67 *chase*: Dispel.

    mantle: Cover.

68 *clearer*: Gradually clarifying.

70–71 *pay thy graces | Home*: Fully reward your virtues (or services).

74 *pinched*: Tormented.

76 *remorse and nature*: Pity and natural feeling.

81 *reasonable shore*: Edges of their reason (imagined as a seashore, gradually being filled by the waters of understanding).

85 *discase me*: Remove my magician's robes.

86 *sometime*: Formerly.

88–94 *Where the bee sucks . . . hangs on the bough*: For Robert

Johnson's setting of this song, see The Music, pp. 91–3.
It expresses Ariel's delight in the freedom which he
knows he is about to achieve.

90 *couch*: (1) Sleep; (2) lie close, crouch.

96 *So, so, so*: Prospero adjusts his new ducal costume.

101 *presently*: At once.

102 *drink the air*: From the Latin *viam vorare*, 'to devour
the road, travel quickly'.

103 *Or ere*: Before.

111 *Whe'er*: Whether.

112 *trifle*: Trick.
abuse: Deceive.

116 *crave*: Require.

117 *An if this be at all*: If this is actually happening.

118 *Thy dukedom I resign*: Antonio is Duke of Milan, but
since he is a tributary of Naples, Alonso controls the
dukedom and its succession, which he here returns to
Prospero.

119 *my wrongs*: The wrongs I did to you.

123–4 *do yet taste | Some subtleties*: Still feel some of the illu-
sions. 'Subtleties' also meant ornamental pastries, which
could be literally 'tasted'.

126 *brace*: Pair.

128 *justify*: Prove.

129 *No*: Sebastian is amazed that Prospero knows their
secrets, and puts it down to demonic possession, but
Prospero's single word retorts that what he says is the
truth. This encounter introduces complicating notes
into the ending: neither Sebastian nor Antonio expresses
any remorse, Prospero forgives Antonio through
gritted teeth and his brother says nothing in reply.

131 *infect*: Pollute.

133–4 *perforce I know | Thou must restore*: Because Alonso has
already declared as much.

139 *woe*: Sorry.

140–41 *patience | Says it is past her cure*: Fortitude is unable to
heal it.

145 *late*: Recent.
supportable: Endurable. Prospero is saying that Alonso

still has his daughter to comfort him, whereas, having
'lost' Miranda, Prospero is now on his own.

150 *That they were*: If it would make it possible for them
to be there.

154 *admire*: Wonder.

155 *devour*: Swallow up (implying they stand around open-
mouthed).

156 *do offices of truth*: Function truthfully.
their words: 'Or that their words' is implied.

163 *of day by day*: To be told over many days.

167 *abroad*: Anywhere else.

171 *discovers*: Reveals (by pulling aside a curtain in front
of the central space at the rear of the stage).

172 *play me false*: Are cheating me. The lovers talk between
themselves and do not notice the court party until 178.

174–5 *for a score of kingdoms . . . call it fair play*: To Ferdinand's
claim that he would not cheat her for the world, Miranda
jokingly retorts he would do it if twenty kingdoms were
on offer – and still she would forgive him. This exchange
introduces another complicating note into the ending,
though it can be staged as innocently playful love-talk.

176 *vision*: Illusion.

176–7 *one dear son | Shall I twice lose*: Because he will be
snatched away from me again.

180 *compass thee about*: Surround you.

186 *eld'st*: Longest.

187 *Is she the goddess*: Like his son at I.2.421–2, Alonso
takes Miranda for a supernatural being.

190 *I chose her when I could not ask my father*: Alonso's
consent would be necessary to his son's choice of
marriage partner.

191 *one*: A living father.

193 *renown*: Report.

196 *hers*: Her father too.

200 *inly*: Inwardly.

205 *Was Milan*: Was Prospero.

207–8 *set it down | With gold on lasting pillars*: Gonzalo refers
to the architectural monuments, such as Trajan's
column at Rome, that celebrated the achievements of

Roman emperors and their successors. He begins by acknowledging the political dimension of the marriage, that Prospero's descendants will not merely be dukes but kings.

214 *still*: Forever.

his heart: Anyone's heart.

219 *That swear'st grace o'erboard*: Whose swearing drives God's grace off the ship. In fact, the only people to use swear-words in the opening scene were Sebastian and Antonio.

223 *three glasses since we gave out split*: Three hours ago (calculated by the hourglass) we reported wrecked.

224 *yare*: Seaworthy.

226 *tricksy*: Full of tricks.

227 *strengthen*: Increase.

232 *several*: Various.

236 *trim*: Garments (or perhaps equipment).

238 *On a trice*: In an instant.

240 *moping*: Bewildered.

241 *diligence*: Diligent one.

244 *conduct*: Director.

246 *infest*: Trouble.

247–50 *At picked leisure ... These happened accidents*: When, soon, we find a suitable free moment, I myself will privately explain these incidents to you, so as to make their likelihood apparent.

256 *Every man shift for all the rest*: In his drunken state, Stephano reverses the usual sense of this idiom.

257 *Coragio*: Italian, 'courage'.

258 *bully*: Term of endearment.

259 *If these be true spies which I wear in my head*: If I can believe my eyes.

261 *Setebos*: The god worshipped by Caliban's mother, see I.2.373.

262 *fine*: Splendidly dressed.

264–6 *What things are these ... no doubt marketable*: Antonio and Sebastian react to Caliban exactly as Stephano and Trinculo have done, taking him for a fish and speculating on his value as a commodity.

badges: Insignia. Noblemen's servants at this time wore badges which identified who their employers were.

And deal in her command without her power: Sycorax could exercise some of the moon's authority (over the tides), but did not have her full power (or, did not have her real power).

272–3 *this demi-devil ... he's a bastard one*: Cf. Prospero's account of Caliban's parentage at I.2.319–20.

275 *own*: Take responsibility for.

275–6 *I | Acknowledge mine*: At its simplest, Prospero is saying that, unlike Stephano and Trinculo, Caliban belongs to his household, but the remark seems to suggest that he feels responsible for Caliban's defects, or that Caliban embodies some negative element within his own nature.

280 *gilded 'em*: Made them flushed.

281 *pickle*: Predicament. But Trinculo takes 'pickle' to mean the process by which meats are preserved by being soaked in alcohol – which is why he has no fear of *fly-blowing* (= becoming rotten).

289 *sore*: (1) Painful; (2) pathetic.

293 *As you look*: In so far as you hope.

294 *trim*: (1) Prepare; (2) clean and decorate.

296 *grace*: (1) Favour; (2) forgiveness.

306 *particular accidents*: Individual events.

312 *Every third thought shall be my grave*: For Prospero's paradoxical awareness that he loses his power even in the act of reassuming it, see Introduction, pp. lxi–lxiv.

314 *Take*: Captivate.

316–17 *shall catch | Your royal fleet far off*: Enable you to overtake your fleet (which has set off back to Naples, I.2.232–5).

317 *chick*: Term of endearment.

319 *Please you draw near*: Prospero invites the other characters to enter his cell, though these words can be addressed to the audience, as a transition into the Epilogue. The effect of the Epilogue will be different depending on whether Prospero speaks for the company or remains onstage alone.

Epilogue

1 *my charms are all o'erthrown*: Referring to Prospero's abandonment of his art (V.1.50–57), but also to the actor reaching the end of the play.

4 *here*: (1) In the island; (2) in the theatre.

7 *the deceiver*: Antonio.

9 *bands*: Bonds.

10 *of your good hands*: Your applause, which, being noisy, will break the spell.

11 *Gentle breath*: The audience's supportive praise for the play.

12 *project*: Cf. V.1.1.

13 *want*: Lack.

16–18 *Unless I be relieved . . . frees all faults*: The primary reference is to the Epilogue itself, and its plea that the audience should be merciful towards any *faults* in the performance, though Prospero's theological language also positions him as a sinner pleading for forgiveness on the Day of Judgement (a more serious meaning reiterated in the final couplet).

20 *indulgence*: Favour; but there is a more specific meaning in Catholic doctrine, in which priests could grant 'indulgences' to benefactors of the church, reducing the time that, after death, they could expect to spend in purgatory as a punishment for sin.

Read more in Penguin

PENGUIN SHAKESPEARE